D0929817

Southern Baptist Politics

Arthur Emery Farnsley II

Southern Baptist Politics

Authority and Power
in the
Restructuring
of an
American Denomination

The Pennsylvania State University Press
University Park, Pennsylvania

Library of Congress Cataloging-in-Publication Data

Farnsley, Arthur Emery.
    Southern Baptist politics : authority and power in the restructuring of an American
denomination / Arthur Emery Farnsley II.

        p.   cm.
    Includes bibliographical references and index.
    ISBN 0-271-01001-0 (alk. paper)
    1. Southern Baptist Convention—Government—History.   2. Democracy—
Religious aspects—Southern Baptist Convention—History.   I. Title.

BX6462.8.F37   1994
286'.132—dc20   93–6039
                                                                          CIP

Published by The Pennsylvania State University Press,
Barbara Building, Suite C, University Park, PA 16802-1003

It is the policy of The Pennsylvania State University Press to use acid-free paper for the
first printing of all clothbound books. Publications on uncoated stock satisfy the minimum requirements of American National Standard for Information Sciences—Perma-
nence of Paper for Printed Library Materials, ANSI Z39.48–1984.

Contents

Acknowledgments

Teachers have always occupied a special place in my life. The occasion of my first book, which marks the end of the educational credentialing process, seems the appropriate place to thank those on whose shoulders I stand: Juanita Cauble, Henry Poteet, Richard Wardell, John Richardson, Denny Hall, Jim Dieckman, Donald Baker, Bert Stern, David Greene, the late Eric Dean, David Kelsey, George and Violette Lindbeck, Jon Gunnemann, Frank Lechner, and Steven Tipton. I hope that each will, at least in some way, find my efforts here worthy of all of their efforts.

Three teachers deserve my special thanks. Paul Harrison has never met me, and it is not his fault that I used a book he wrote more than thirty years ago as my starting point. Nonetheless, he consented to read my manuscript (as a member of my dissertation committee) and offered his advice. I have run a great risk by inviting comparisons to his work, but he had the grace not to make such judgments himself.

It would not suffice simply to list Bill Placher among my teachers—he is my friend and confidant. I would call him my teaching role-model, but I fear that damns him with faint praise. Bill represents all that is best in the tradition of liberal education, even if he would occasionally rather not.

"Thank you" hardly covers my debt to Nancy Ammerman. My work as her research assistant provided me with much of the data presented here. She has been my boss, my teacher, my dissertation director, and, in our most recent project, my research colleague. Although Nancy is the "mentor" for many aspiring teachers and scholars, I will always think of myself as her apprentice. Without her unswerving support and her confidence that I had something important to add to the conversation, I would never have had the nerve to write a book on the same general topic as her award-winning *Baptist Battles*.

As my manuscript developed into a book, I learned a great deal from two new teachers, Peter Potter and Peggy Hoover, my editors at Penn State Press. Their careful reading, polite suggestions, and constant encouragement improved the manuscript considerably.

I could not have received the wisdom of my teachers without the support of my family. I cannot thank them all by name here, but I cannot fail to acknowledge both the subtle and concrete ways by which my wife—Gail Fotheringham Farnsley—made all of this possible. Some academic trails wander off into confusion and obscurity. Gail, with help from our daughters, Sarah and Caleigh, keeps me on the straight and narrow most of the time.

Finally, two men—John Stuart Gibson and Arthur Emery Farnsley—were both teachers and family. Their political savvy, sturdy faith, and plain common sense have always been my inspiration. This book is dedicated to the memory of my grandfathers.

Introduction

Denominations have been the essential form of American religious organization. They embody many of the notions—volunteerism, pragmatism, utilitarianism, individualism, populism, democracy, and even laissez-faire—that define the American character. Major changes in the denominational landscape may signal shifts in religious ideas and attitudes, but those changes also serve as signposts marking important themes in the wider, secular culture. The most important of these changes in the past two decades has been the transfer of power and leadership in America's largest Protestant denomination, the Southern Baptist Convention.

The recent controversy in the Southern Baptist Convention (SBC) is a familiar topic. Few religious disputes have generated the secular publicity of the SBC feud. At the 1989 annual meeting of the SBC in Las Vegas, both major wire services were represented, as were local newspapers from across the South. Local television crews came from as far away as Atlanta. A serious ideological and theological dispute in an organization claiming 15,000,000 members was clearly newsworthy.

If the 1989 meeting demonstrated the broad appeal of this story, the 1990 meeting in New Orleans signaled its end. The election of a fundamentalist presidential candidate that many moderates thought beatable, and the withdrawal of most denominational funds from the Baptist Joint Committee on Public Affairs (BJCPA) marked the beginning of a new era for the Southern Baptist Convention. The 1991 meeting in Atlanta, which included a visit from President Bush, showed no signs of denominational controversy.

As the dust settles, clearer contours of the change emerge. In the fray of battle, it was sometimes difficult to see anything but the individual combatants and their weapons. Now, perhaps, the story can be viewed through the much wider lens of American culture and politics. The SBC cannot be put back together as it was. However, both the SBC of the future and other denominations can benefit from asking what happened here and why.

The basic story is simple enough: religious conservatives, usually referred to as fundamentalists, wrested control of the denomination's hierarchy and bureaucracy from the more moderate faction that had led the denomination for years. The denomination's corporate programs are now operating within the context of a philosophy of biblical inerrancy. The old bureaucratic establishment, represented most conspicuously by the several seminaries the SBC operates, was attacked and changed. Most of the former leaders now operate outside the formal channels of SBC cooperation.

No story can be reported as a simple rehearsal of actions and dates. The terms "feud," "fundamentalist," "control," "inerrancy," and "attack" suggest a confrontational interpretation that many participants once hoped to deny. Those terms suggest unavoidable polarization and separation.

Both academics and the media have described the situation as a "conflict." Nancy Ammerman goes so far as to call her comprehensive social study *Baptist Battles*.[1] In that book, she develops a detailed social history of the SBC. Joseph Barnhart emphasizes theological differences.[2] James Hefley stresses political, ideological, and even personal differences, from the conservative point of view.[3] Ellen Rosenberg focuses on the denomination's particular, southern, cultural context.[4] Bill Leonard provides a historical and cultural study from the perspective of a moderate insider.[5]

The media, as one might expect, has paid much attention to powerful individual personalities and to policy decisions that refer to matters of ongoing public debate.[6] The similarities between the rise of the fundamentalists

1. Nancy Ammerman, *Baptist Battles: Social Change and Religious Conflict in the Southern Baptist Convention* (New Brunswick, N.J.: Rutgers University Press, 1990).

2. Joseph Barnhart, *The Southern Baptist Holy War* (Austin: Texas Monthly Press, 1986).

3. James Hefley, *The Truth in Crisis: The Controversy in the Southern Baptist Convention* (Dallas: Criterion Publications, 1986). Hefley has now contributed several volumes in this series, adding annual updates to his original journalistic efforts.

4. Ellen Rosenberg, *The Southern Baptists: A Subculture in Transition* (Knoxville: University of Tennessee Press, 1989). Although Rosenberg focuses on the denomination's cultural context, there is reason to believe that she fails to understand it in many important respects. Her generalizations that southerners are "chauvinistic" and "hyper-racist and -sexist" (p. 13) pose questions about her ability to treat the SBC objectively. See also John Eighmy, *Churches in Cultural Captivity* (Knoxville: University of Tennessee Press, 1972), for a related discussion.

5. Bill J. Leonard, *God's Last and Only Hope: The Fragmentation of the Southern Baptist Convention* (Grand Rapids, Mich.: Eerdmans, 1990).

6. For instance, the *Atlanta Journal and Constitution* often covers stories concerning the ordination of women, the acceptance of homosexuals, or employment of divorced people as

within the SBC and the emergence of a larger New Christian Right (NCR) in national politics have been suggested often if never well documented.[7]

Although there is widespread agreement that the changes stem from different sources of conflict—cultural, theological, and ideological—this agreement alone does not explain why the changes took a distinctly political shape. The world is full of all sorts of conflict rooted in every conceivable source. Why was *this* conflict resolved by appeal to proceduralism and party politics? *This book intends to answer those questions. It intends to explain the "political" nature of this conflict by reference to both secular and ecclesiastical polity.* Whatever lessons about denominations may be learned from this episode must be found somewhere in that complex organizational matrix.

Perhaps the best reason to define the conflict and its resolution as political is that most Southern Baptists now define it that way themselves. Most fundamentalists (who prefer the term "conservative") and most moderates (who once wanted to be called "centrists") will tell you that there was little *theological* difference between the presidential candidates offered by either party in the later years of the controversy. All of them were biblical inerrantists with conservative social views on such issues as abortion. All of them were important preachers from large churches. All emphasized personal evangelism and "soul-winning." They differed, Southern Baptists will say, primarily on their views of polity and policy: Should the denomination employ non-inerrantists? Should the seminaries teach historical-critical method? Should mission funds be spent on education and health as well as on evangelism? Should the opinions of a minority in the denomination be considered when making policy decisions, and to what degree? These are the questions that have separated Southern Baptists, and most of those Baptists describe these questions as political despite their theological or ideological or cultural underpinnings.

Another reason to call the conflict political is nearly as significant: the SBC developed two recognizable parties, each of which fielded an identifiable slate of candidates for office. Moreover, something very like platform planks were circulated at annual meetings through the media organs (SBC

---

missionaries. One wire-service writer at the Las Vegas meeting was particularly interested in the resolution concerning apartheid, although most Southern Baptists themselves (and most others in the newsroom) considered this to be a peripheral matter.

7. The 1991 meeting in Atlanta made the connection between the New Christian Right and the SBC difficult to refute. Between the Pastor's Conference and the actual meeting, the guest list included President George Bush, Lieutenant Colonel Oliver North, Tim LaHaye, Charles Colson, and Jerry Falwell.

Today and *The Advocate*) of the two parties. These developments so closely resemble the partisan politics associated with city, state, or national elections that any outside observer—perhaps especially an outside observer[8]—would call them "political" in the everyday use of the term.

Calling the conflict "political" does not, of course, say anything substantive about it, nor does it show who might benefit from that designation. Politics will be defined here along liberal[9] lines as an arena bounded by procedural norms for establishing and maintaining group governance. That definition points toward a study of the *procedures*, both formal and informal, that underlie political activities in the SBC. How the polity has changed and how those changes were accomplished are the kinds of questions whose answers will most benefit both Southern Baptists and members of other denominations.

The Importance of Procedure and the Arenas of Conflict

Procedural analysis does not need to be excessively theoretical or abstract. In this case it will unfold within a narrative history of the denomination's polity in order to identify the points at which key changes occurred. The story of the politicization of the SBC is, in one way, a simple narrative: Why was the polity created as it was, and what forces prompted changes in it through the years. The SBC is an organization, but it comprises several smaller organizations. Each of these has specific functions and goals. Good procedural analysis must explain the relationship of these smaller units to one another and to the whole.

Explaining changes in organizational polity also means explaining the *power* and *authority* within that polity. Authority, in this context, means the *institutional legitimation* for one's actions. People with authority lead because they are *authorized* to do so. Power, by way of contrast, refers to *the means* to act. People with power act because the action is available to them whether they have authority for it or not.[10]

---

8. Southern Baptists have a stake in downplaying the recognizable political structures they have developed and emphasizing instead their common fellowship.

9. In my analysis, the word "liberal" will be used in its classical sense, referring to individual autonomy, freedom, and responsibility. Occasionally the more contemporary "conservative-traditional" (liberal-progressive) distinction will be necessary because it was used so frequently by the participants themselves. I hope the two senses can be kept analytically separate.

10. The seminal work on this subject as it relates to my research is Paul Harrison's *Authority*

The SBC comprises several different kinds of formal and informal power and authority that are interconnected in a variety of ways. This study emphasizes the four kinds that most shape this religious organization: democratic, bureaucratic, charismatic, and legal (scriptural). Although it would be tempting to limit this "political" analysis to the democratic, or perhaps the democratic and the bureaucratic, such a move would surely fail. Power and authority among Southern Baptists cannot be understood apart from the presence of the charismatic pastor and leader. Furthermore, the authority of scripture, a kind of legal authority, lies at the very heart of this political controversy.

Charting the development of political *procedures* for dealing with different tensions within an organization illuminates both the causes and the likely effects of those tensions. The Southern Baptist Convention, long a kind of populist collective, emphasized democratic elements already in its polity in order to deal with the stress caused by increasing diversity and pluralism among its membership. It did this by developing—and later discarding—a formal two-party system that closely resembled the one associated with secular politics in the United States. That system generated organizational change by expressing the will of the membership in more explicit terms and by changing the definition of "member" altogether. The SBC limited the theological spectrum from which it would draw participants and, in the process, created at least one shadow organization, which now operates independently. All of this occurred, moreover, in a climate of decreasing denominational rigidity in the nation as a whole.

This complex story develops on several levels at once. On one level it is a historical narrative. Why was the polity created as it was, and what forces prompted changes in it through the years? On another level, the story of politicization is about the interplay between power and authority in different contexts. Democratic, legal/scriptural, charismatic, and bureaucratic authority carry different weight in different settings. These ideal-types must also stretch to fit a wide range of historical events and empirical analysis.

Every story is a collection of related details played out against a much broader backdrop. A subtle but dramatic change in the understanding of ecclesiological power converged with a renewed emphasis on democracy and populism in the SBC. That convergence makes sense only when viewed

---

and Power in the Free Church Tradition: A Social Case Study of the American Baptist Convention (Princeton: Princeton University Press, 1959). Although Harrison deals with American Baptists, the ways in which his analysis is relevant to Southern Baptists, and the ways in which it is not, are important topics to which I shall return at length.

against the backdrop of cultural and political changes in the wider South and in America as a whole.

Although each ideal-type of authority plays its own role in this drama, the tension between democracy and bureaucracy takes center stage.[11] Highlighting this tension points up the most pressing issues faced by Southern Baptists themselves, who saw this battle as a fight among constituents over what course the denomination's corporate programs would take. The dual requirements of bureaucratic efficiency and maximum participation make these two loci of authority ultimately, and inevitably, the most important ones. Charismatic power and the legal authority of scripture must never be forgotten in a discussion of Southern Baptists, but this analysis stays close to the rather orthodox Weberian assumption that they will, in the long run, assist rather than prevent or outstrip formal and procedural norms. All of these forces together have shaped a new constituency that will hold the Southern Baptist leadership continuously accountable.

American Pluralism: A Model for Change

The "new constituency" is the thread that runs throughout, holding the pieces together.[12] If this is a story of change in different contexts, then that change must itself be guided by something. Two types of social changes—the spread of the SBC beyond the "solid South,"[13] and the modernization[14] of the South itself[15]—have precipitated other changes, and conflicts, in the SBC. The turmoil in the SBC cannot be understood apart from the context of increasing pluralism and diversity in its membership. Although the de-

11. The best early discussion of this comes from Max Weber, who describes the ways in which democracy must create bureaucracy for reasons of efficiency, even though bureaucracies have several traits that are decidedly undemocratic.

12. See Nancy Ammerman, "The New South and the New Baptists," *Christian Century*, May 14, 1986, pp. 486–88.

13. This is a term usually credited, in this context, to Samuel Hill, to whom I'll return.

14. "Modernization" is a troublesome term that many have chosen to abandon. Nonetheless, there is an identifiable movement toward urbanization, industrialization, pluralism of values (often associated with cosmopolitanization), and secularization, which can be deemed "modernizing" with sufficient conceptual accuracy.

15. On this point, an interesting book is John Egerton, *The Americanization of Dixie, the Southernization of America* (New York: Harper & Row, 1974). Mark Shibley tests Egerton's hypothesis, and concludes it is valid, in his recent "Southernization of American Religion: Testing a Hypothesis," *Sociological Analysis* 52, no. 2 (1991), 159–74.

nomination is a large enough organization that it can act on its environment as well as react to it, its current controversy *is* primarily reactionary; it is a response to changing social circumstances that are beyond its control.[16]

Analyzing religious change within the wider social context is a well-established practice that recalls the classic literature on church and sect.[17] The SBC provides an interesting twist on the church/sect hypotheses because the SBC is generally regarded as more of a church-type denomination in the South—where it is part and parcel of its culture—but more like a sect (or at least outside of the "mainline") in other regions of the nation. Thus politics in the SBC can be viewed within the framework of church-sect tensions typical of American denominations so long as one recognizes the apparent paradox: as this denomination's cultural context has become more diverse, and as it has therefore been forced into a more sect-like stance, the denomination has also developed institutional procedures that are decidedly more church-like, at least in the sense that the church depends more on procedural, rather than charismatic or legal, control.

The SBC thus illustrates two concurrent trends in American religious life: the pull toward greater privatism and greater sectarian division between the righteous and the damned, and the pull toward what might be called public or civil religion, interested in protecting and increasing membership and participation.[18] As the denomination type itself draws on church-like and sect-like tendencies,[19] so has this particular denomination's struggle highlighted the tension always present in this unique religious form. And if the American religious scene underscores the problems and the promise of the denomination type, the SBC illuminates with peculiar clarity the underlying American commitment to individualism and democratic, popular participation that permeates all American institutions, including religious ones.

It would be rash to infer too much about all denominations from this one, recent, tumultuous decade in Southern Baptist life. Nonetheless, such a significant change in America's largest Protestant denomination sends up a flare that cannot be ignored. Theories of religious organization have always

16. This claim probably belies my own preference for certain kinds of secularization arguments despite their current disfavor among sociologists. Later I argue what I can only state here.

17. Although I do not want to discount mysticism or deny that such a category might be useful here, I am presently more interested in the evolved literature on sectarian movements.

18. Robert Wuthnow, *The Restructuring of American Religion* (Princeton: Princeton University Press, 1988).

19. See Bryan Wilson, "An Analysis of Sect Development," *American Sociological Review* 24 (February 1959), 3–15.

observed the link between religious organizations and their culture. The story of political change in the SBC suggests helpful ways to refocus that vision. More important, however, is the message to other denominations and to the SBC of the future. This historic battle within the SBC offers crucial lessons about power, authority, membership, and organization in the American religious context.

All religious organizations in America will be facing major cultural and demographic changes as they enter the twenty-first century. Conflict will follow. In each case, the group's particular polity and history will confront other cultural assumptions about social power and organizational change. The Southern Baptist case, as every other, represents a unique convergence of a specific case and a broader cultural context.

The transfer of power in the SBC marks the first time that fundamentalists have succeeded in gaining power in a major denomination. It also sets a startling precedent for the mobilization of political resources to settle theological and ecclesiological disputes. The SBC *is* a specific case and it *would* be rash to infer too much from its turmoil. Given the importance and the distinctiveness of this case, however, it would be equally rash to dismiss this story as an isolated, historical accident. The postconflict SBC, along with every other large religious organization, must now evaluate the implicit *assumptions* of its polity in the context of expanding pluralism and an increasing awareness of political strategies for creating change.

1

Growth in Organization and Agreement, 1845–1941

Becoming a Denomination

Understanding contemporary Southern Baptist polity requires a basic familiarity with the Convention's roots.[1] Such a familiarity requires, in turn, a clarification of certain vague but widely held notions about the denomination's history.

One popular explanation for the "unity" is emphasized in the names of current American denominations (e.g., Lutheran Church in America, United Methodist Church, Presbyterian Church USA, United Church of Christ). According to this explanation, many of these groups were united before the Civil War. Just before (or during) the war, they split over slavery, and in the twentieth century they reconciled. Southern Baptists, however, have yet to reconcile with Northern Baptists (later to become the American Baptists), and the two remain separated halves of an antebellum whole.[2]

1. I capitalize "Convention" when referring to the organizational entity formed by the many congregations that make up the SBC. The denomination is "the Convention." I use the lower-case "convention" to refer to the annual meeting of messengers from the Convention. For instance, the 1991 "convention" was in Atlanta.

2. I do not mean that this was the road traveled by the other denominations named, but

The problem with such a description, as it applies to Baptists, is that there was never one, unified denomination in the early nineteenth century that could be split. Instead, there were—following centuries of Baptist insistence on religious freedom and local organization—autonomous churches gathered in geographic associations, which had formed separate benevolent societies for the purposes of forwarding common missionary goals. Chief among these societies was the General Missionary Convention, a group that formally began doing foreign mission work in 1814. Though many Baptists certainly wished to bring all cooperative benevolent work under the canopy of this convention (a movement that threatened, at the turn the century, to supersede local associations), such a centralizing effort ultimately failed.[3] Baptist benevolences, including most notably The Baptist General Tract Society and The American Baptist Home Mission Society, remained, like the General Missionary Convention, independent bodies connected to autonomous local churches that were affiliated only by region and local association. In short, these large, national organizations remained societies, as their names denote, and not associations.

Indeed, a denomination that understood itself as such came into being only in 1845 with the advent of the Southern Baptist Convention. Thus the problems that separated Baptists in the mid-nineteenth century—usually involving but never limited to the practice of slavery—did not divide a unified denomination but created one. It is only when Southern Baptists withdrew from their older involvements in the mission societies that they attempted to create a unified denomination capable of carrying on several different kinds of benevolent work under one banner.

Southern Baptists recognized that such a centralized denomination would be more efficient and more powerful. William Johnson of South Carolina, credited with creating this new polity, went so far as to call such a concentrated effort "of the first moment in all combinations of men for important enterprises."[4] There was, however, no precedent for Baptist consolidation in so large a region; indeed, there was an open suspicion, grounded in those centuries of Baptist insistence on religious liberty, of any attempt to centralize power or authority. Johnson and the other founders surely shared such

that this is the popular explanation for the relatively recent "mergers" in these supposedly main-line groups and for the Baptists' "failure" to consolidate.

3. For nearly a century, the General Missionary Convention was as close as Baptists got to a denomination. See Robert Baker, *The Southern Baptist Convention and Its People, 1607–1972* (Nashville, Tenn.: Broadman Press, 1974), pp. 105–13 (hereafter cited as Baker, *SBC*).

4. See ibid., p. 165.

suspicions. Therefore they proposed an organization that would not supersede the local congregation. Said Johnson:

> In its successful operation, the whole Denomination will be united in one body for the purpose of well-doing, with perfect liberty secured to each contributor of specifying the object or objects, to which his amount shall be applied, as he please, whilst he or his Delegation may share in the deliberations and control of all the objects, promoted by the Convention.[5]

Of course, it is difficult to discern immediately any meaningful differences between this new denomination and the older society structure. Though all mission efforts would now be coordinated through one central body, the funds for these efforts could still be designated and even withdrawn at the local congregation or association's discretion. And funds were definitely the issue: representation in the new convention was determined solely on the basis of financial support. Further, any local body could entirely withdraw from this Convention as easily as the South had withdrawn from the various national societies earlier in the century.

But there were differences between the older societies and the new Convention. This awkwardly organized group was now formally an association with one overarching institution—embodied in the triennial, "democratic" meetings—responsible for the several separate boards it comprised. Despite its loose organization, the Convention gained strength for a time. The "society-type" of independent, designated funding reassured Baptists who wanted to do cooperative mission work without becoming a centralized denomination, while the "association" type of unified structure gave the new organization both financial and numerical clout.

But the obvious tensions this loose arrangement could cause were already beginning to surface.[6] The earliest period of Southern Baptist life, from 1845 to about 1890, must be understood in terms of this tenuous alliance and the organizational strain it created. As the Convention came to be understood as a centralized association—its Foreign Mission Board and Domestic and Indian Board, the key reasons for the Convention's existence, were joined

5. Ibid. (from Robert Baker, A Baptist Source Book [Nashville, Tenn.: Broadman Press, 1966], p. 114).
6. Baker (SBC, p. 176) notes this tension. Harrison, Authority and Power, makes good use of the technical distinction between "society" and "association" and of the inherent tension when the two are fused.

by the Bible Board in 1846 — the tension between its dependence on voluntary, designated contributions and its "democratic" style of government grew. Questions about selecting delegates based only on financial contributions troubled the many churches whose contributions were small; at the same time, the emerging Landmark movement continued to question the theological correctness of any decision-making body beyond the local church.[7] The rapid numerical growth of Southern Baptists through the Civil War pointed up the pressing need, and the eventual failure, to confront the questions of polity and of representation head-on.

Such questions were neither rhetorical nor matters of theological quibbling. In the aftermath of the Civil War, the various boards of the Convention suffered deeply. In the South, both the ideological debate concerning society and association and a general postwar scarcity led several state organizations to use the bulk of their state's resources to operate their own programs, neglecting the cooperative efforts. In the North, existing missionary societies — including those societies once sponsored by Southern Baptists — challenged their new, southern counterparts. By the turn of the century it was clear that Southern Baptists would need either to recognize some central authority and commit themselves to cooperative work, or to return to their earlier society structures.

Thus from its earliest days the new denomination experienced the organizational tension between "church" qualities and "sect" qualities, as they would later be defined by Troeltsch.[8] It wanted to be unified and to develop an organizational form capable of giving it shape and guidance, but at the same time it clung to the idea of independence and personal charisma. This first period of Southern Baptist saw a stark contrast between the two, bridged only by a weak notion that growth demanded some movement away from pure sectarianism.

7. The Landmark movement, "begun" by J. R. Graves of Tennessee (see William Barnes, *The Southern Baptist Convention, 1845–1953* [Nashville, Tenn.: Broadman Press, 1954], which also cites J. M. Pendleton and A. C. Dayton, p. 103), has come to symbolize Baptist insistence on the priority of the local congregation. (Barnes's book is cited hereafter as Barnes, SBC.) Historically, "Landmarkers" insisted that membership is only in a local congregation and that the sacraments of baptism and communion should only be performed there both for and by members. One was a communicant in one's local church only, and one was to be baptized there and only by someone who had been baptized "correctly" — by immersion. The Landmarkers' attempt to establish a historic succession of "properly baptized believers" from Jesus to the present created many interesting historical problems. Any authority vested in a larger body is considered unscriptural, though voluntary cooperation by many local groups is permitted. Note here too the crucial importance of the distinction between an association and a society.

8. Ernst Troeltsch, *The Social Teaching of the Christian Churches*, trans. Olive Wyon (1911; reprint, Chicago: University of Chicago Press, 1960).

Organizational Cohesion, Democratic Roots, and the Advance of Bureaucracy

By 1890 such a return was unlikely. Though beset with financial and ideological problems, the Southern Baptist Convention continued to develop as an organization in the postwar years. Its earliest and most important boards had assumed, in rough fashion, the shape (if not the scope) they maintain today: the Foreign Mission Board (FMB, 1845), the Home Mission Board (HMB, originally the Domestic and Indian Mission Board, 1845) and the Sunday School Board (SSB, originally the Bible Board, 1851).[9] Lay missionary groups, such as the Women's Missionary Union (WMU, 1888 — although it adopted this name in 1890), were in place, and the Laymen's Missionary Movement (LMM, 1906) was soon to follow.[10] Southern Baptist Theological Seminary (SBTS) in Louisville (moved from Greenville in 1877) was soon to be followed by Southwestern Baptist Theological Seminary (SWBTS, 1908) in Fort Worth, as a training ground for men (and women) approaching the Baptist ministry.[11]

But if the Convention had, by the turn of this century, come too far as a complex organization to return to the days of independent mission societies, it had not come far enough to sponsor any long-term, permanent programs within its broad institutional base. There were no guarantees of regular receipts or even of any region's continued support. Indeed, it was not until 1906 that the Landmarkers largely abandoned their efforts to pull Baptists away from such a large organization altogether.[12] There was no direct connection between the various boards and lay groups except for the designation "Southern Baptist" and the triennial, then biennial (1851), then annual (1866) meetings of Southern Baptists from which they ostensibly directed the many boards. There was no predictable, regular continuity in funding, membership, or authority. In short, the 1845 vision of a united denomination had been realized in name but not in substance at the nineteenth century's end.

9. The body that controlled Sunday School operations was, for a time, subsumed under the auspices of the Home Mission Board.

10. The LMM does not exist now as such, although a Brotherhood Commission has arisen in its place.

11. Baker (SBC, p. 303–4) points out that Southwestern was coeducational from its founding, much of its funding having been raised by the women of Texas.

12. Barnes (SBC, p. 167) marks the withdrawal of many Landmarkers in 1906 as a key point in the journey toward consolidation.

This turn-of-the-century period, between 1890 and 1920, marked a formalization of Southern Baptist polity, which soothed some of the old tensions between individual and corporate efforts but raised new tensions in their place. Being beyond the point of returning to missionary societies, but well short of Johnson's original goal, Southern Baptists had no choice but to strengthen their central organization. The many functions of their institution, represented by its many boards and programs, required some form of central leadership. Now largely unencumbered by the Landmark movement's loud dissension, in 1913 the Convention created a "Commission on Efficiency" to study "the organization, plans and methods of this body, with a view to determine whether or not they are best adapted for eliciting, combining and directing the energies of Southern Baptists and for securing the highest efficiency of our forces and the fullest possible enlistment of our people for the work of the kingdom."[13] As Baker remarks, this was denominational talk.

In 1916 the Commission on Efficiency recommended the creation of a strong Executive Board. Though Baptists, predictably, wanted to limit the Executive Board's powers to organizing the annual meetings and advising the various boards when requested to do so, they empowered it, pragmatically and yet fatefully, to "act ad interim on such matters as may arise pertaining to the general business of the convention and not otherwise provided for in its plan of work."[14] The Southern Baptist Convention was now a continuing, permanent organization with a central authority capable of overseeing the many institutions it comprised.

Of course, a more central and recognizable locus of power only highlighted the existing problem of representation. If there was concern about participation in the decision-making process before, when the Convention existed only as a group of specific institutions under the direction of an infrequent assembly of participants, such concern could only increase as the Convention became an entity unto itself, above and beyond the various boards.

The more power and authority the Southern Baptist Convention claimed, the more its constituents would require definition of their roles in the decision-making process. The more cooperative work tended toward bureaucratic or "committee" authority, the more Baptists were going to insist on democratic participation.

13. *Proceedings of the Southern Baptist Convention, 1913* (published annually by the Executive Committee of the SBC), pp. 69ff.
14. *Southern Baptist Convention Annual, 1917* (published annually by the Executive Committee of the SBC), pp. 33ff.

Such insistence met little opposition because, generally speaking, everybody agreed. Southern Baptists were committed to democratic governance of their cooperative efforts. But agreeing on democracy in principle, and working out a clear plan for institutionalizing it, are two different things; the Convention's inability to complete the latter successfully plagues it even today.

Baker notes that "almost every year between 1877 and 1917 someone raised the question from the floor of the Convention relative to changing the method of representation."[15] In fact, the Convention did tinker with various possible methods—representation by association, by state, by number, and by church. But which body would be represented was not the only question. Were these to be "delegates," chosen by local churches to represent them at a gathering (this was the choice of the Landmarkers), or "designates," chosen to represent Baptists in general but with no authority either from or over the group from which they came. Fearing that the use of the term "delegates" suggested that these people could speak *for* members of their group (and thus threaten the Baptist insistence on liberty) or that the Convention could then justifiably exercise authority *over* those who were thus represented (therefore threatening local autonomy), Southern Baptists chose the "designated" method. Groups could send "messengers" whom they would designate to speak as Baptists, but not necessarily for their group.

The question of which bodies could send groups simply was not answered in the early part of the century. Any "Baptist body" could send one messenger for each $250 it contributed, with one representative to be elected from each district association. Annual meetings were not technically "representative," with delegated power over any churches, but simply gatherings of Baptists expected to reach a denominational consensus.[16] The new and more powerful central body was still linked, however awkwardly, to the Baptist tradition of democratic participation. As long as the anticipated Southern Baptist consensus remained intact, there were no foreseeable problems. Messengers would point a direction, and the Executive Committee, boards, and programs would act accordingly on the Convention's behalf.

This new polity signaled that many of the church-like tendencies of the denomination were holding sway. The radical sectarianism of the Landmarkers had been repulsed. The structures were in place for providing an educated clergy and for operating some central bureaucracy. The sectarian

15. Baker, SBC, p. 314.
16. Ibid., pp. 314–16.

tendency to insist on independence and full democratic participation was checked by successful growth of membership and programs. But if this polity seemed to work smoothly for a while, it is probably because problems seldom appear at the center, but rather at the limits, of consensual power and authority.

Settling In: The Limits of Denominational Solidarity

A test of those limits was not long in coming. By 1920, only four years after the formation of the Executive Committee, the strengthened Convention was about to suffer its first theological and institutional storm. A period of consolidation and organization was about to face its first serious disorganizing pressure.

Biblical inerrantists within the Convention, most colorfully (if not most accurately) personified by J. Frank Norris of Fort Worth, mounted an aggressive challenge to the newfound "centralizing" tendency and to the perceived "modernism" or "liberalism" that accompanied it.

Of the two, centralization and modernism, it is difficult to say which Norris and the biblical inerrantists—popularly known as fundamentalists[17]—liked least. Norris broadly criticized even the suggestion that any body beyond the local church should have ecclesiastical authority. Though virtually any history of the Southern Baptist Convention describes the "Seventy-Five Million Campaign," begun in 1919, as the benchmark of the new, powerful denomination,[18] Norris described it as "dictatorial, unscriptural, [and] a foolish waste of hard-earned Mission money." Norris frequently described the denominational authorities as "the Sanhedrin" and called the Baptist World Alliance, with which the Convention casually cooperated, "the biggest cuckoo framework ever among Baptists."[19]

17. By "fundamentalism" I mean the inerrantist movement at the turn of the century commonly characterized by Bible conferences, the teachings of Scofield, and the pamphlets "The Fundamentals." Among the classic works on the subject are George Marsden, *Fundamentalism and American Culture: The Shaping of Twentieth-Century Evangelicalism* (New York: Oxford University Press, 1980); Ernest Sandeen, *The Roots of Fundamentalism: British and American Millenarianism, 1800–1930* (Chicago: University of Chicago Press, 1970); and Norman Furniss, *The Fundamentalist Controversy, 1918–1931* (Hamden, Conn.: Archon Books, 1963).

18. It is interesting to note that the campaign failed. It quickly generated $92 million in pledges, all budgeted for increased denominational programming. Because of another postwar scarcity and a nation-wide skepticism of foreign missions that followed World War I, however, its postwar receipts of $58 million left the denomination deeply in dept.

19. Quoted by C. Allyn Russell in his excellent biography of Norris in *Voices of American Fundamentalists: Seven Biographical Stories* (Philadelphia: Westminster Press, 1976), pp. 36ff.

His views concerning modernism and liberalism within the convention were equally subtle. He was convinced that Southern Baptist educational institutions—most notably his alma mater, Baylor—were teaching the heretical doctrines of historical-critical method in biblical interpretation and, perhaps even worse, Darwinian evolution. He claimed that he personally forced eight professors from Baylor's faculty, calling them "anthropoid apes" who taught "animal ancestry." Norris publicly challenged the theological opinions of several Baptist leaders, including the esteemed George Truett of First Baptist in Dallas, whom he called "the Infallible Baptist Pope" and "The Great All-I-Am"—among other things, undoubtedly. Norris refused to use the denomination's too-liberal Sunday School material and announced that his church would teach "the Bible only." When Southern Baptist leaders attempted to censure him and restrict his participation in the Convention, he held rallies of his own opposite the Baptist General Convention of Texas and the Southern Baptist Convention. Finally, unable to maintain even a nominal association with the Convention, Norris withdrew and formed his own "fellowship" of churches in 1931.[20]

It is popular among Baptists of all stripes today, both "moderate" and "fundamentalist," to discount Norris and to disavow connection to his fiery militancy. But if he was an extreme, even singular, proponent of the conservative position, that did not make the position itself any less widely held. The fundamentalist movement that was spreading across America had deep roots in the Southern Baptist Convention.

Indeed, most Baptists were probably closer to the theological and biblical beliefs of Norris than to those of his enemies. In the 1920s the Convention repeatedly reaffirmed its "consensus" on biblical infallibility and its disapproval of the Darwinian hypothesis,[21] going so far as to adopt a sort of "confession of faith" in 1925. This was, they insisted, not intended as an authoritative creed or a binding statement of belief, but as a statement of denominational consensus. The skepticism with which many Baptists greeted this "confession," however, indicated that they had not abandoned their insistence on individual autonomy. Though they agreed, basically, with the theological views of the fundamentalists, they were not willing to insist on the conformity to "orthodox" doctrine that most fundamentalists outside the Convention considered necessary.[22] Therefore, while fundamen-

20. Ibid., pp. 30–40.
21. In 1925 the Convention adopted the view of E. Y. Mullins, who argued that science could not deny, and was not even necessarily relevant to, theological belief. See Baker, *SBC*, pp. 398ff.
22. Robert Torbet, *A History of the Baptists* (Philadelphia: Judson Press, 1950), p. 443.

talist inerrancy "succeeded" in the Convention insofar as it was the dominant theological view, fundamentalism as a militant, antimodern movement failed because, frankly, there were too few opponents to maintain widespread interest.

This does not mean that the fundamentalist movement disappeared. Throughout the 1920s the Convention's annual meetings housed spirited debates concerning the need for a formalized doctrine, heresy among missionaries, and "liberalism" in the seminaries.[23] But in nearly every case the inerrantist position was heard, nominally accepted, and then dissolved into a nonbinding resolution such as the confession mentioned above. Only a crisis of "biblical" proportions could have shaken most Southern Baptists from their love of autonomy and soul-competency such that they would have been willing to "impose" any sort of mandatory sanctions. So the fundamentalist movement was not defeated, but quieted, and 1930 found Baptists much where they had been in 1920.[24] The center had held; the "consensus" was still strong enough to guide the growing denomination.

And the denomination did grow. The period from 1920 to 1941 need not be finally characterized as a time when fundamentalism first raised a mighty challenge, but as the time when the new bureaucracy proved itself capable of withstanding disorganizing pressure. It was a time of settling in, when the new establishment proved that it was, indeed, established.

In the mid-1920s the Executive Committee's powers were broadened in order better to integrate the Convention's many scattered programs. At nearly the same time the Convention established its financial "Cooperative Program" aimed at channeling all funds into a single treasury for centrally determined distribution. Though the "society"-type of fund designation was imbedded deeply enough in Southern Baptist life that specific designation of funds was still allowed, the move to a cooperative financial structure, with budgets to be drawn by the Executive Committee, clearly signaled acceptance of a less qualified or restricted national program. In essence, the denomination now had funds with fewer strings attached.

This new round of centralization created, inevitably, a new call for a better structure of representation. The commitment to democracy requires that every move to consolidate power or authority be accompanied by a reciprocal move to clarify participation by the larger constituency. In 1931 the process

23. Sydney Ahlstrom, A Religious History of the American People (New Haven: Yale University Press, 1972), p. 913.
24. Ibid.

for choosing Convention representatives was refined somewhat. Under the new system, any church cooperating with or friendly to the Convention could send one messenger. This placated populist sentiment that poor churches were being ignored by the larger body. In addition, a church could send one additional messenger for every 250 members or $250 it donated to the Convention's cooperative efforts up to a maximum of ten messengers. This rewarded larger or more "cooperative" churches for their success and support without making it possible for any enormous or very wealthy church to exercise too much control. These "messengers" were still to be regarded as *designates*, speaking as Baptists in an attempt to reach fraternal consensus, and not as *delegates* with any authority either from or over their churches. Therefore, while the old Landmarkers' insistence on the priority of the local congregation won the day, their wish for delegates did not. Though the new method for determining participation in the process was more precise, the process itself was still structured to achieve consensus and not to balance competing interests.[25]

Such consensus was likely to be ever more difficult to determine. The new method of representation, coupled with rapid numerical growth in the denomination, meant that literally thousands of people were now eligible to attend the annual meetings. It was clearly impossible for these gathered messengers any longer to run the workings of the Convention. Fortunately, they did not need to do so. By the early 1930s the Convention was already putting in place an extensive system of boards and committees that would actually do the Convention's work at the national level. In addition, numerous responsibilities were assumed by the leadership in the various state conventions. The result is what Baker calls "dual representation":

> One on a state basis being penultimate in authority, aristocratic in make-up, widely representative, consisting of state membership as trustees on boards, commissions, committees, and institutions; the other being the Convention session itself—ultimate in authority, democratic in make-up, totally available for members of all cooperating churches, and less representative because of the size and place of the annual meeting, economic conditions, and the intensity of issues confronting the Convention, etc.[26]

25. See Baker, SBC, pp. 404–5, for a full discussion of the new "messenger" policy, from which my own discussion is taken.
26. Ibid., p. 408.

The shape of denomination was now cast. It was to be democratic, to be sure, but as in all large democracies most constituents are only symbolically represented both at the level of designated messengers who speak for all Baptists and at the level of a bureaucracy which acts, day-to-day, on behalf of the whole. This shape has been modified, but essentially unchanged, up to the present.

As the Convention grew numerically and financially, its bureaucracy grew with it. This third, "settling in," period of Southern Baptist life set the course for its polity. The organization that less than a century earlier had *no* substance, no center, was now a living, breathing entity. Its Foreign Mission Board, Home Mission Board, and Sunday School Board—the Convention's mainstays (and the descendants of the nineteenth century missionary societies)—were joined by an Annuity Board (AB) in 1918. The Convention was now stable enough to offer continuity and stability to its constituent pastors. It added the New Orleans Baptist Theological Seminary (NOBTS, 1925) to Southwestern and Southern.

Besides these large organizations, the Convention developed several commissions to deal with various pieces of Southern Baptist life. These included the Brotherhood Commission (formerly the Laymen's Missionary Movement) and the Historical Commission (1936), whose purposes are evident in their titles.

Such a large bureaucratic structure called for an even stronger central leadership. This role was filled, predictably, by the Executive Committee and by a network of seminary and agency trustees. The Executive Committee, whose numbers grew through years of denominational growth, assumed the role of "board of directors" for the denomination. This group assumed primary responsibility for creating a budget and dispersing "cooperative" funds to the various boards and agencies. Needless to say, the day-to-day operations of the Convention became more and more removed from the direct leadership of the messengers at annual gatherings. In fact, Southern Baptists were learning, through the practices associated with "settling in" if not by conscious choice, that board and committee and commission memberships were the key to influence in denominational life. The Convention's "consensus" was now "represented" in the form of board directors, trustees, and committee members.

Of course, the annual gathering could not take direct responsibility even for membership in the various organizations. In recognition of this they established a Committee on Committees (with two members from each cooperating state), to be appointed by the Convention's president on a rotating basis, to represent the denomination as it picked its representatives. This committee would name, among other things, a Committee on Boards (also two from each state), which nominates the trustees who actually control the day-to-day activities, including hiring, of the agencies and seminaries.

Even with such bureaucratic refinements, however, ultimate responsibility for these nominations, at least at the very top levels, such as the Executive Committee and the Committee on Committees, had to rest somewhere. Further, that responsibility had to have some connection to the democratic participation at the annual meetings. Historically such responsibility had rested with the Convention president, who was elected at each annual meeting. The post was once mostly honorary, given to a man who was not expected to be a Convention CEO but a pastor, usually of a large and influential church. His job was not to run the Convention but to suggest names of people who would. As the denomination grew in numbers and in financial resources it was forced to develop a powerful bureaucracy, and accordingly presidential power of appointment took on larger and larger dimensions. Though the Convention, following its historic suspicion of the concentration of power, moved to limit the terms of office of the president, the committee members, or the trustees, the Convention had already decided—almost by default—where its true denominational power would rest. The designated messengers would, by passing resolutions (a sort of group opinion) and electing presidents, help establish a bureaucracy and offer the Convention a general direction. The bureaucracy would then implement the Convention's wishes in concrete, material ways.

This, therefore, is the polity that Southern Baptists carried into the middle of the twentieth century. Though their annual meetings are democratically run, it would be difficult to call the Convention a democracy even in the broad sense used to describe western republics such as the United States. There, every citizen may vote for representatives and on some "referendum" issues of corporate importance, even if many choose not to do so. Further, the representatives are responsible to and for their districts or states and vote the interests of their constituents. That this type of polity often falls short of its goal is not the point here; it is intended to achieve them.

The polity of the Southern Baptist Convention is not representative. It is based on the participation of *designated* messengers who speak not for their constituents but merely "as Baptists." The model is not one designed to give voice to and to determine between competing interests, as western "democracies" are usually designed to do, but to generate and validate consensus.

In its first hundred years, the SBC moved from being a loose coalition and became an established, centralized organization. As a denomination, its sectarian qualities—charismatic leadership, independence, and reliance on local autonomy—gave way to the more church-like qualities of central organization and the regularization of procedures and norms. The move was far from fluid, but the drive for efficient operation was able to guide the denomination despite ideological opponents and the ever-present insistence that each move to centralize control be checked by a corresponding move to ensure democratic, local participation in the decision-making process, that every move toward the churchly be met with a corresponding assurance of sectarian freedom. The tension between these two types of trends—democratic versus bureaucratic, independent versus coordinated, church versus sect—was in the subsequent years subjected to environmental pressures unimaginable at the turn of the century.

2

Diversity, Disagreement, and Organizational Tension, 1942 to the Present

Transcontinental Expansion and the Roots of Pluralism

Its establishment settled, the denomination began to move and to expand. This fourth period, beginning in 1942, comes amid what Baker calls "revolution."[1] The Southern Baptist Convention more than doubled its membership in the years from 1942 to 1972.[2] It also greatly expanded its geographical reach.

The choice of the year 1942 is not random for Southern Baptists. In that year, California's general convention was recognized by the SBC over the protests of many northern Baptists. As California most clearly represents the nation's westward expansion, so does its inclusion in the Convention signal a move beyond the Deep South and the Southwest and a new, national constituency.

As Baker points out, the Convention added only six states from its incep-

---

1. Baker (SBC, p. 412) uses this term to suggest the social upheaval that began in 1942 and included the bombing of Hiroshima and Nagasaki, the Korean War, and the Southeast Asian conflicts.

2. From approximately 5,400,000 to 12,100,000 (ibid., p. 413). The later benchmark here is 1972, because it was the end of Baker's study.

tion in 1845 until 1942. In the thirty years that followed, it added bodies in all thirty of the other states as well. The Convention could (and would) still correctly be called "Southern Baptist," but its membership could no longer be counted on to think or act or vote only as southerners.

This is not to say that the Convention automatically lost its ability to generate, and to be governed by, consensus. In the new states even more than in the South, the appellation "Southern Baptist" said something about one's theology and ecclesiology. One might be born Southern Baptist in Georgia and might remain Southern Baptist, perhaps within a different congregation, even if one's views or ideas changed. In the south, Southern Baptists were a cultural constant, but in California or Oregon or Michigan, "Southern Baptist" was a conscious identification that one could not take lightly. There people were Southern Baptist not by accident of birth but because they wanted to be.

So certain characteristics of the SBC remained constant: it was theologically and biblically conservative, culturally southern, and still organizationally centered. It added Golden Gate Baptist Theological Seminary (GGBTS, 1944), Southeastern Baptist Theological Seminary (SEBTS, 1951), and Midwestern Baptist Theological Seminary (MWBTS, 1957) during this expansion period. The bureaucratic machinery of the Convention seemed up to the task its own success continued to set for it.

It created several new commissions during this period, including the Radio and T.V. Commission in 1956 and the Stewardship Commission (begun in 1958 and officially recognized in 1961). If the functions of these bodies are evident in their names, perhaps less obvious is the purpose of the Christian Life Commission (CLC, 1953), which took on the responsibility of educating Baptists, and others on their behalf, concerning the upright Christian life.[3] Among their many concerns historically have been liquor laws, gambling, civil rights, divorce, and crime, to name a few.

The denomination also named two standing committees—the Committee on the Denominational Calendar (1948) and the Committee on Public Affairs (CPA, 1939, although the name was changed to this in 1950)—to conduct Convention business. The Calendar Committee sets such things as meeting dates and special observances, which is of no small importance in a group that does not observe the liturgical calendar. The CPA, later the Public Affairs Committee (PAC), represents the denomination on the Baptist Joint Committee on Public Affairs (BJCPA). The BJCPA is an umbrella

---

3. Begun as the Social Service Commission, the CLC assumed its new name in 1953.

group for many Baptist organizations (and therefore is not a Southern Baptist body) that operates out of Washington, D.C. This group's historic mandate has been to disseminate public affairs information, protect religious liberty, and foster a spirit of church-state separation, long a Baptist benchmark, in the nation's capital.

As with the BJCPA, the Convention is associated with, but not directly responsible for, the Baptist World Alliance (an international group), the American Bible Society, and the Women's Missionary Union (WMU). Though often regarded as an auxiliary unit (not unlike the Eastern Star in Freemasonry), the WMU is a fully independent mission group whose fund-raising efforts have often been, for most Baptists, the most visible incarnation of both home and foreign missionary activities.[4]

The denomination, as a large bureaucratic organization, thrived on its consensual power base. Cooperative Program, Sunday School Board, and mission offering receipts grew into the tens, then hundreds, of millions of dollars, and predictably the agencies and boards grew with them. The Annuity Board currently has in excess of $1 billion and is growing steadily. In addition, each state convention has a significant (though much smaller) operating budget. Salaries for agency staff are small compared with the secular, corporate world but large compared with the average Southern Baptist pastor.

"Who makes what" is, of course, not the issue here. More important by far is the realization that the denomination had indeed become a thing unto itself. If its problem was once its inability to establish a central base of operations, its problem is now a growing concern that its centralization has become excessive.[5] The sheer size of the denomination's financial resources is one source of concern; its increasing tendency to locate important agencies and staff in Nashville, Tennessee, is another. The framers of the denomination's polity envisioned a regional denomination with offices located throughout the south: the Foreign Mission Board in Richmond, the Home

4. The two mission offerings any Baptist could name—the Lottie Moon Christmas Offering for foreign missions and the Annie Armstrong Offering for home missions—are both named for women and often directed by women in local congregations. Indeed, Annie Armstrong is literally a founder of the denomination, having led the Convention to appoint "lady delegates" and having directed the WMU in the late nineteenth century.

5. Much fundamentalist rhetoric is intended to arouse populist sentiment against "overgrown bureaucracy." Said one fundamentalist organizer, "Generally speaking, when you get a big bureaucracy the most important thing about it is that it perpetuate itself. They'll tolerate anything so long as it's not divisive and does not threaten the bureaucracy. So I think that's the way liberalism started getting in."

Mission Board in Alabama (later Atlanta), the first seminary in Greenville (later Louisville), and the Sunday School Board in Nashville. In the 1920s the new Executive Committee opted to locate in Nashville along with several small agencies. When they were joined by the Historical Commission, and when all of these groups were moved to a location actually adjacent to the Sunday School Board, a sort of "Baptist block" had been created.

What developed, at least according to conservative critics of the denomination (both within and without), was a large-scale bureaucracy staffed by organizational professionals. Though the Landmarkers themselves were long gone from the denomination by mid-century, their concern for local church autonomy and for a decentralized cooperative effort remained. No "true Baptist" would be willing to cede authority—the *right* to govern granted by the governed—to these denominational professionals, but the volume of money they stewarded and their proximity to the decision-making process made it impossible to deny them the power to govern in fact.[6]

Such power, in and of itself, was enough to worry many Southern Baptists. Every move to enlarge the power of the Executive Committee or to "deregulate" Cooperative Program funds met with resistance.[7] But for an ever more vocal segment of the Southern Baptist population, the problem was not simply a matter of sheer organizational power, but also a matter of who held it.

Denominational employees were drawn from the educated middle class of Southern Baptists. They were aware of such national political trends as those toward integration and women's rights and, though they were generally conservative, they could not help being influenced by their cultural environment. Similarly, though virtually all Baptists remained biblically conservative, the segment of the population most exposed to "modern" political trends was also exposed to "modern" biblical theory, such as "historical-critical method" or "higher criticism." The denomination's central institutions began to reflect—at least according to conservative, biblical inerrantists—a more "liberal" viewpoint than the denomination as a whole. The conservatives, or fundamentalists, became the standard-bearers of the sec-

6. The Weberian distinction between these, to which I will return, is the central element in Paul Harrison's seminal work *Authority and Power in the Free Church Tradition* (1959). Authority is, generally speaking, an institutional license to decide or act because one was elected or appointed specifically to do so. Power, by contrast, is the ability to decide or act based on proximity—accidental or intentional—to the levers necessary to effect such changes.

7. The best history of these two institutional components and their relationship is Albert McClellan, *The Executive Committee of the Southern Baptist Convention, 1917–1984* (Nashville, Tenn.: Broadman Press, 1985). By "deregulate" I mean to distance further the denomination's funds from specific designation by the giver(s).

tarian, independent viewpoint that stood always ready to challenge the centralizing, formalizing tendencies of the denomination.

Thus the unresolved tension of the 1920s resurfaced. Baptists were to tolerate different points of view and to recognize the authority of each local congregation, but were committed, both formally and informally, to the absolute authority of scripture. [8] The difficulty in maintaining these two positions heightened another existing tension, that of representation. Differing views of scripture had threatened to undermine the "designated messenger/consensus" model before. It was not easy for rigid fundamentalists and those who opposed any enforcement of "doctrinal orthodoxy" to achieve "consensus." To these two tensions was added a third, the product of a growing organization: Baptists were to love cooperation but to fear centralization. Church-like organization, sectarian independence, and a biblicism that promoted both individual interpretation and doctrinal correctness were forced to stand side by side. As the three tensions intermingled, it was obvious that something had to give.

Unsettling: A Challenge to the Old Establishment

In 1961 something did give, marking the beginning of the fifth period in the history of Southern Baptist polity.[9] Broadman Press, the publishing arm of the Sunday School Board, published Ralph Elliot's *Message of Genesis*. Elliot, a professor at Midwestern Seminary, took the position that many of the stories related in that book were parabolic, intended to "convey deep historical insight" but not to recount actual, historic events.[10] Though this position was common, indeed standard, among biblical scholars at university-related seminaries, it was not the position of most Southern Baptists. At the 1962 annual meeting, the Convention passed resolutions affirming faith in the entire Bible as authoritative and opposing views that might undermine its historical accuracy or doctrinal integrity.[11] Though Midwestern Seminary

8. The idea of biblical authority could be used to bolster both a more church-like and a more sectarian stance, depending on one's view of latitude in interpretation. The fundamentalists, here the champions of independence, would later be accused of using the scriptures in a more doctrinal, church-like manner.

9. Because his book ends at 1972, Baker's final period is from 1942 to 1972. Given the huge changes that began in 1979, it now seems preferable to end the period beginning in 1942 at 1960, recognizing 1961 as the beginning of the present conflict (although the institutional change does not really begin until the election of Adrian Rogers in 1979).

10. Ralph Elliot, *The Message of Genesis* (Nashville, Tenn.: Broadman Press, 1961), p. 15.

11. Baker, *SBC*, p. 416.

initially stood behind their professor, they eventually dismissed him when he declared he would seek another publisher for *The Message of Genesis* when Broadman declined to reprint it. This controversy prompted a call for a reassertion of the traditional biblical beliefs of Southern Baptists. A committee of state convention presidents, headed by Herschel Hobbs, drafted a new "confession" known as the Baptist Faith and Message. Though this confession was, as earlier ones had been, nonbinding and without mandatory authority, it reaffirmed that the Bible was the inerrant, divinely inspired word of God. The key phrase stated that the Bible "has truth without any mixture of error for its matter."

Such a statement did not end the inerrancy controversy, however. Also in 1961 the Sunday School Board was planning a twelve-volume set called "The Broadman Bible Commentary." When the first volume, which included Genesis and Exodus, appeared in 1969, it was as if the Elliot controversy was born anew. In 1970 the Convention's annual meeting voted overwhelmingly (by a margin of more than 2 to 1) to withdraw and rewrite the volume. The board did this, asking the same authors (G. Henton Davies of Britain and Roy Honeycutt of Midwestern Seminary, later president of Southern Seminary, respectively) to revise their contributions, giving consideration to the conservative viewpoint. This did not satisfy conservatives, who voted in 1971 (this time by a much narrower margin) to instruct the board that its wishes had not been carried out. The board then changed authors for the Genesis segment, but not without stating that it believed it had carried out the Convention's wishes in the first place, and not without selling the original volumes in Britain.

These two, very similar, incidents point out the growing tension within the Convention. Not only had biblical inerrantists reasserted their opposition to any liberalized reading of scripture, and their numerical clout within the denomination, but they had also pitted themselves against the denomination's institutions. Though it would at first appear that they had "won" in both of these conflicts, they were not so sure. In both cases, the organization involved attempted to maintain the status quo while seeking to meet the convention's instructions: Midwestern did not immediately dismiss Elliot, and the Sunday School Board did not immediately change authors; in both cases the authors involved refused to capitulate, and the changes were made grudgingly by the entities involved.

Indeed, inerrantists within the Convention were not at all convinced that Midwestern Seminary or the Sunday School Board had acknowledged that a problem of fair representation of Baptist viewpoints existed. And the problem was not confined to literature concerning biblical criticism. Other Southern Baptist agencies, most notably the Christian Life Commission (CLC), sponsored programs that were unsatisfactory to inerrantists. Indeed, in 1970 the Convention seemed poised to dismantle the CLC at the same time it was chastising the SSB. Only a plea from several prominent pastors, including Herschel Hobbs, averted such an action.[12]

Such pleas were becoming commonplace. James Hefley, a conservative journalist who has chronicled the controversy in the SBC, characterizes the plea of the establishment within the denomination as one for "unity amidst diversity." Biblical conservatives were being asked to recognize that there were Southern Baptists of all types representing all ranges of biblical interpretation. They were being asked to be tolerant of ideas different from their own.

It is obvious, however, that such pleas were falling on suspicious ears. If representatives of the establishment thought they were saying "There is room for all views of scripture in the Convention," inerrantists were hearing "There are rooms for all views of scripture but we do not intend actually to teach or to publish yours." In short, both the SSB and the seminaries were influenced by—and felt themselves responsible to—a broader and more liberal constituency. They were willing to cooperate with inerrantists in Convention activities such as home and foreign missions, but they were not willing, in the view of the inerrantists, to seek a "representative" balance in their faculties or publishing lists.

Organizing a Fundamentalist Coalition

It was in the aftermath of the second "Genesis" controversy, in the early 1970s, that the inerrantists decided to organize. Several of the leading pastors representing this biblical viewpoint met in Atlanta at the First Baptist Church, where Charles Stanley was pastor. They started a movement that was named "Baptist Faith and Message Fellowship," and they founded a periodical, to be edited by Bill Powell, called *The Southern Baptist Journal*. The discontent that had surfaced in the 1920s and again in the 1960s now had a focus and a voice. It was not to be easily silenced or ignored again.

In fact, the *Journal* was seldom silent, and usually much too loud to be

12. Ammerman, *Baptist Battles*, p. 68.

ignored. Powell openly attacked those whom he perceived as liberals, asking them pointed questions about their beliefs concerning key literalist shibboleths, such as the "historicity" of the biblical story of Adam and Eve. He promoted the "alternative" Baptist seminaries, notably Mid-America Seminary in Memphis, Tennessee (founded in 1972 in Little Rock, now adjacent to Bellevue Baptist Church, where Adrian Rogers is pastor); the Criswell Biblical Studies Center (founded in 1971, affiliated with the First Baptist Church of Dallas, where W. A. Criswell was pastor); and the Luther Rice Seminary (founded in the 1960s as a "correspondence" school for biblical conservatives).

Much as the Convention had done in the late nineteenth century, the inerrantists were building an institutional structure complete with schools and publications. The key figures were inerrantist pastors: Adrian Rogers (Memphis), W. A. Criswell (Dallas), James Draper (Euless, Texas), Bailey Smith (Del City, Oklahoma, and later Atlanta), Jerry Vines (Rome, Georgia, and later Jacksonville), and Charles Stanley (Atlanta). They began speaking together at evangelism conferences and meetings concerning "inerrancy." Though they were supported in their efforts by such non–Southern Baptists as Jerry Falwell, the real thrust of the movement came when they began to receive the public support of such Southern Baptist laypeople as Judge Paul Pressler of Houston.

Pressler, a graduate of Phillips Exeter Academy and Princeton University, had long been a conservative critic of the "liberal drift" in the seminaries and the increasing centralization and corporatization in the denomination. After the Elliot controversy he wrote a pamphlet, "A Message to Southern Baptists," trying to alert the Convention to the direction he saw the denomination taking. Although he spoke to many conferences and meetings, there is little mention of him in Baptist discussions before the late 1970s. Although he was a member of the Baptist Faith and Message Fellowship, he was dissatisfied with their methods and withdrew quickly.[13] It was apparently not until well after his meeting with Paige Patterson, then a student at New Orleans seminary and later an associate pastor at the First Baptist Church of Dallas and then president of the Criswell Center for Biblical Studies, that any real political organization began.

As a judge, Paul Pressler was intimately familiar with both secular politics

13. Related by Pressler in a very public discussion with Richard Jackson at the Executive Committee meeting in Nashville on February 22, 1989. There is little outside evidence available to corroborate, or challenge, this claim.

and strict attention to legal details. Though other Southern Baptists had been involved in "political" groups such as the "Religious Roundtable" (Charles Stanley and Ed MacAteer, a member of Adrian Rogers's Bellevue Baptist, for example), no concerted effort to apply political strategies to the Southern Baptist Convention had yet been attempted. Though the biblical inerrantists had won every vote on scriptural issues that came to the floor of the annual meeting, they believed these victories had done little to change the way the denomination conducted its business. Pressler, along with Patterson, determined that substantial changes could be made if the "conservatives" could organize effectively with an eye toward the key "decision-making" centers of the denomination: the trustees of the various agencies and the Convention's very powerful Executive Committee.[14] After a reported meeting at the Atlanta airport with several of the key pastors from the Baptist Faith and Message Fellowship, the Pressler-Patterson coalition (as it is commonly called by "moderates" within the denomination and even by conservative journalist James Hefley) began to make its bid to change the denomination's leadership.

Although not all of this organizing was a matter of public record (the Atlanta airport meeting is nearly impossible to verify in any detail), neither was it unseen by the rest of the denomination.[15] The unrest that began in the early 1960s was clearly growing, and denominational moderates, including those within the agencies, were anxious to calm the coming storm. Though W. A. Criswell had been president of the Convention in 1969 and 1970, he was not elected as a result of any particular political effort. He was an inerrantist, to be sure, but he was also pastor of the largest Southern Baptist church in the world and was revered as a great preacher and soul-winner; his election was very much in keeping with the Convention's historical record of electing important southern preachers to its highest post. By the mid-1970s, however, moderates and establishment types within the denomination were beginning to see the signs of the more organized movement, inspired but not actually led by Criswell, which posed a much greater threat. They hoped specifically to thwart, according to C. R. Daley of Kentucky, the political ascendance of Adrian Rogers.[16]

To do this, the moderates turned in 1976 to the highly esteemed James

14. "Firestorm Chat," taped interview with Judge Paul Pressler conducted by Christian Reconstructionist Gary North and distributed widely in fundamentalist circles by Dominion Tapes.

15. Hefley does cite this meeting in his *Truth in Crisis*, vol. 3 (1988), p. 14.

16. Ibid., p. 62.

Sullivan, the recently retired head of the Sunday School Board. He was elected president but refused a second term. To replace him, the moderates chose Jimmy Allen—or, as some would have it, he chose himself. In a highly publicized (after the fact) lecture at Southern Seminary, C. R. Daley called Jimmy Allen the first to "announce" his candidacy and to ask for support.[17] Allen won the presidency of the Convention at the annual meeting in 1977 in a runoff with Jerry Vines of the Baptist Faith and Message Fellowship (they had both outpolled Richard Jackson of Phoenix, another inerrantist, to earn a spot in the runoff). In 1978 Allen was elected for the customary second term. It was the last time a moderate or "establishment" candidate would win the Convention's presidency.

By 1979 the "Pressler-Patterson" coalition was running at full strength. Both Pressler and Patterson were speaking at local churches and at evangelism conferences, and while neither endorsed any candidate for Convention president it was widely believed that the standard-bearer for their "cause" would be Adrian Rogers.[18] The moderates' earlier fear of Rogers was not unfounded: he was pastor of the Convention's second largest church; Mid-America, perhaps the leading "independent" seminary for Southern Baptists, was located at his Memphis, Tennessee, church; his congregation's connections to the New Christian Right were well known; and he was a compelling speaker. Despite his repeated protestations that God had not called on him to run, Rogers decided in an eleventh-hour prayer meeting that his candidacy was proper. Though six men were nominated for Convention presidency (not including Allen, because the Convention's constitution limits the term to two consecutive years), there was no split like the Vines/ Jackson split in 1977: Rogers was elected on the first ballot. The stage was now set for historic changes in the denomination's major institutions.

Of course, those changes would be slow in coming. Though the president did get to make the nominations for the Committee on Committees, which nominates the Committee on Boards, which nominates trustees for the various agencies, each step of this process takes a full year. Add to that time-lag the fact that trustees and Executive Committee members have rotating

17. The inerrantists have made much of the fact that the moderates "started" the current political controversy by citing this lecture. Historically, the election of Convention president was not a heated or bitter matter. Many candidates, recognized as able pastors, were nominated, and one was selected for the "honor," often after several ballots. Daley is quoted by Hefley as saying that using a retired editor's lecture shows the "desperation of the fundamentalist faction" and that he knew there were fundamentalist "spies" in the hall and expected his lecture to wind up in the "war room" in Dallas.

18. Hefley, *Truth*, pp. 65ff.

terms of office and that it becomes clear that any major change in agency policy takes a sustained effort over several years. The conservatives, not satisfied with the effects of their earlier victories on Convention motions and resolutions, seemed willing to wait. And such willingness implied a great confidence that they could in fact sustain their momentum for as long as necessary.[19]

Their confidence was not misplaced. In 1980 Adrian Rogers declined to run for his second term and was replaced by Bailey Smith, an Oklahoma pastor and later evangelist who was closely associated with Jerry Falwell.[20] Smith was reelected in 1981. In 1982 and 1983 James Draper of Texas was elected. In 1984 and 1985 it was Charles Stanley of Georgia. In 1986 and 1987 Adrian Rogers assumed the mantle again, and in 1988 and 1989 Jerry Vines of Florida served. All of these men were known inerrantists supported by both Pressler and Patterson.

The Establishment Strikes Back

This succession of power was not as smooth as its continuity might imply. When Stanley was elected in 1984, the controversy seemed to reach a boiling point. At the annual meeting that first elected him in 1984 in Kansas City, there were roughly 17,000 messengers. This number was in line with the general convention attendance since 1952.[21] At the 1985 annual meeting in Dallas, however, there were 45,519 messengers, almost exactly twice the

19. Many moderates showed a corresponding confidence that the fundamentalists could not maintain momentum. Said Glenn Hinson: "Despite Rogers' remarkable first ballot triumph, he came out with no mandate to do what his fundamentalist backers hope he will do—expel from seminaries and other agencies all who don't subscribe to biblical inerrancy. . . . Southern Baptists, while conservative, don't get really lathered up over 'orthodoxy.' They went through one of these crises before, in the 20's when J. Frank Norris and his fundamentalist movement tried to do what Harold Lindsell (author of *The Bible in the Balance* [1979] . . . and editor of *Christianity Today*) is doing now. It took awhile, but they soon got tired of the Norris sideshow and set their face forward with renewed confidence in their institutions" (Glenn Hinson, "Southern Baptist Fundamentalists Stirring up a Storm," *Christian Century*, July 18–25, 1979, pp. 725–27).

20. It is in fact Smith, not Falwell, who made the infamous comments about the size of Jews' noses and about God not hearing the prayers of Jews.

21. The first annual meeting to have more than 10,000 messengers present was in 1952. Since that year the meeting has usually drawn between 10,000 and 20,000 messengers, with a low of 8,871 in Portland, Oregon, in 1973 and a high of 22,872 in 1978. The average for 1952–84 was 13,967 (*Southern Baptist Annual, 1988*).

highest number that had ever attended previously. It was obvious that the moderates were prepared to react to the conservative surge and that conservatives were equally (or better) prepared to meet them.

Why moderates chose this annual meeting cannot be determined definitively, but several points are worth noting. First, they had an announced candidate from Texas, Winfred Moore, who was a known biblical conservative, pastor of a very large church with substantial gifts to the Cooperative Program, and outspoken in his criticism of the "coalition" of inerrantists. The moderates had clearly and publicly not only joined the fray but also admitted that one existed.

Second, Charles Stanley was regarded by many moderates as the weakest of the inerrantist coalition. He had, by some accounts, stolen control of the First Baptist Church of Atlanta. When Roy McClain left as head pastor there, the pulpit committee did not recommend Stanley, his assistant, as his successor. Stanley and his supporters called for a congregational vote, and Stanley was sustained. He was viewed by moderates as autocratic (a charge he did not refute in his handling of the chair at the Dallas meeting) and even unstable.[22] More than that, however, he was not a lifelong Southern Baptist, and his church had been notably uncooperative at all levels, supporting instead independent missions and bible schools.

Finally, the controversy in the state of Texas had not displaced moderates from positions of leadership. Because annual meetings naturally draw disproportionately from the surrounding area, Texas was viewed as a moderate stronghold. The moderates expected to win here, and they made their first concerted effort to attract messengers who would vote to support their candidate and their cause.

Conservatives were not unaware of the vulnerability of their position, but they were not without defenses. They clearly had the better organized and more clear plan of action. They had a strong presence already in Dallas, the home of W. A. Criswell and Paige Patterson; indeed, Dallas is often regarded as the heart of the "coalition" in the Convention. They had an incumbent candidate running for the customary second term, a term that had historically been nearly automatic. Finally, though Stanley was regarded as an independent and a tyrant by some moderates, he was also highly regarded as an evangelist by most Southern Baptists. His sermons were televised nation-

22. The *Atlanta Journal and Constitution* reported that Stanley publicly accused a female church member of being demon-possessed when in 1988 she spoke against the sale of the church's downtown Atlanta property and the removal of the congregation to the suburbs.

wide, and by some estimates he was second only to Billy Graham in exposure and wide recognition within the SBC.[23]

Stanley won in Dallas, but not without accusations of vote fraud, bullying, and registration improprieties. Busloads of messengers had arrived the Tuesday morning of the meeting, voted for the president, and then apparently left. Fearing that moderates might actually vote down the new slate of board and committee recommendations once fundamentalist voters had left, Charles Stanley urged everyone at the Evangelism Conference on Wednesday to return to vote. Said he, "If we lose this, we lose everything."[24] The voting totals after the presidential vote dropped by as much as half. Nonetheless, the conservatives had weathered the storm and had continued their program of appointing committee, board, and trustee members sympathetic to their cause.

Perhaps sensing the uneasiness within the Convention, perhaps truly wishing to reach out in Christian love, and perhaps hoping to silence officially the opposition, the Convention's new leadership made its first intimations of reconciliation at the Dallas meeting. Winfred Moore was elected vice-president by a wide margin, even though there was a candidate from the First Baptist Church of Dallas (motivational speaker Zig Ziglar) on the conservative slate. More important than that, though, the Convention authorized and appointed a Peace Committee to look into the controversy and to report its findings and suggestions for future action in Atlanta the next year.

The 1986 meeting in Atlanta was expected to be even larger than the one in Dallas. Atlanta had hosted the largest meeting ever, before 1985, and was considered the major city accessible to the greatest number of congregations. The moderates were planning to run Winfred Moore again, this time not against an incumbent. Moreover, the Peace Committee had focused everyone's attention on the controversy, and many moderates believed that once

23. The data collected at the Center for Religious Research demonstrated that Stanley was, by a wide margin, the most widely watched of the television personalities associated with the Convention's dispute. Some 27 percent of respondents said they watched Stanley at least once a week, while the next closest personality watched was Jerry Falwell, named by only 12 percent. We did not test for Billy Graham, but it is safe to assume that even Stanley would not approach Graham's level of recognizability.

24. The matter of scores of buses making U-turns that Wednesday afternoon is the subject of moderate jokes but is impossible to substantiate, as is the charge that fundamentalists were handing out stacks of ballots in the parking garage. Paige Patterson's review of Ammerman's book calls such charges "moderate paranoia" ("Help for Confused Baptists," *Christianity Today*, January 14, 1991, pp. 33ff.).

most messengers recognized that a takeover was indeed under way they would seek to restore balance.[25]

The enormous numbers did not materialize, and neither were the moderates' hopes realized. Though Atlanta was by far the second-largest annual meeting ever—40,987—the outpouring of "mainstream" support for the old "establishment" way of doing things was simply absent. The conservatives, alert to the possibility of a moderate coup, supported the candidacy of Adrian Rogers, the candidate in their first organized victory. He won on the first ballot, making it very difficult for observers (and for some moderates) to imagine what circumstances might make a moderate comeback likely. The Peace Committee asked the Convention for more time and was granted it. For the time being they had requested an end to "political" meetings and inflammatory language, citing several recent examples.

The meeting in Atlanta established another trend within the Convention's new politics. The moderates had conceded that they needed a candidate who was biblically conservative; indeed, they turned to an inerrantist. In Atlanta the equally conservative Richard Jackson of Phoenix nominated Moore. Moore and Jackson had established themselves as inerrantists who opposed what they considered "coalition" politics. Other moderates, such as the admittedly more "liberal" Cecil Sherman of Fort Worth or William Self of Atlanta, had recognized that the Convention was biblically very conservative. Their hope was not in an outpouring of support for more progressive theology or programs, but in biblically conservative presidents who would allow room for a diversity of theological positions within the Convention's agencies and seminaries.

To date, those "anticoalition" conservatives have been unsuccessful. Richard Jackson ran against Adrian Rogers in 1987 in St. Louis and was soundly defeated. In 1988 in San Antonio, Jackson ran again against Jerry Vines (a rematch of the first and second runners-up from the 1977 annual meeting). Vines won, but by the narrowest of margins. In 1989 the incumbent Vines won by a more convincing margin (approximately 10 percent) in Las Vegas. In 1990 Morris Chapman won easily in New Orleans, despite some moderates' expectations that he would be a very weak fundamentalist candidate. Chapman won again, this time by acclamation, in Atlanta in 1991.

It was clear after a decade of success that the inerrantist coalition intended

25. It would have been Pollyannaish for the moderates to have hoped for the Peace Committee to censure or otherwise silence the conservatives. However, they could hope for some compromise, or at least for amplification of what they considered "unbaptist" conservative political tactics.

to carry out its program, realizing all of the moderates' worst fears. From the election of Rogers in 1979 forward, each opening on the Committee on Committees, the Committee on Boards, the Executive Committee, and in agency leadership positions and trusteeships have been filled with biblical inerrantists sympathetic to the Convention's conservative movement. At each annual meeting a slate of new members for these entities is presented; as has always been the case, each slate is always accepted. Though moderates have taken to challenging individual names, and even whole slates, the process is usually quick and simple.

The denomination's movement toward "inerrancy" was slowest in the seminaries, doubtless because of the great loyalty academic institutions command and the "inbred" status of their trustees. But change happened there too. Randall Lolley was ousted as president of Southeastern Seminary in 1988, and all of the seminaries, even Southern (long considered the bulwark of the denominational establishment), have begun hiring professors who reflect the inerrantist point of view. A 1987 meeting of seminary presidents in Glorieta, New Mexico, affirmed a conservative position on the Bible that was so close to inerrancy that many moderate supporters were dismayed.

More rapid has been the change in some agency top executives. Larry Lewis, an inerrantist from Missouri, was appointed head of the Home Mission Board. Larry Baker replaced Foy Valentine as head of the Christian Life Commission and was soon replaced himself by Richard Land. Similar changes are to be expected in the other agencies as the rotation of trustees signals an ever-greater inerrantist majority.

Nowhere has the change been more profound or more evident than on the Executive Committee. Because this group meets in Nashville, home to most of the denomination's former establishment, the friction caused by the changes is most evident. Because the Executive Committee holds the purse strings for virtually all of the denomination's cooperative efforts, the change is most profound. Though the annual meeting of the whole Convention has ultimate power to accept or decline the actions of the Executive Committee (and all other entities, for that matter), the Convention has historically accepted the recommendations of its central body. The issues are simply too complex and too wide-ranging to be digested and then acted upon by the thousands of messengers who come for the three-day meetings. Thus the decisions are made, as they have always been, by the few central figures on the key committees, boards, and agencies. If the inerrantists have truly changed the denomination, or if they will be able to do so, it is because they are able to change these key personnel.

Drawing the New Party Lines

Although the fundamentalist coalition has made many changes in the denomination, it would be rash to assume that they have been granted an organizational carte blanche. There are potential limits on the fundamentalists' ability to promote any agenda beyond internal denominational reform.

Moderates had long charged that the biblical conservatism of the fundamentalists was inextricably linked to a political conservatism of the sort identified as "the New Christian Right."[26] They further charged that this political conservatism was hostile to the traditional Baptist prerogative of the separation of church and state. Conservatives, correspondingly, saw political and religious "liberalism" as connected, at least insofar as only biblical liberals could fail to take strong stands against abortion or for school prayer.

The Christian Life Commission, as mentioned above, was long under the suspicion of denominational conservatives, and the coalition changed its leadership when such a change was possible. Richard Land, a fundamentalist fellow-traveler, was chosen to head the Christian Life Commission, and "Foy Valentine," the name of its former "establishment" head, became synonymous with the failure of the denomination's old line.[27]

But the CLC was not the only representative of the denomination to pass through the political arena. As the Convention's voice on moral issues, politics was not even necessarily the commission's primary focus, though its role as the Southern Baptist mouthpiece on social policy was widely accepted. The real Baptist political organ, however, remained the Baptist Joint Committee on Public Affairs (BJCPA)—the Baptist (though not exclusively Southern Baptist, as described above) lobby in Washington.

This was the real Baptist political voice. And this was the voice fundamentalists most wanted to change. It was "political" suicide to question the BJCPA's historic role as guardian of the separation of church and state,[28] but conservative Southern Baptists had long dogged BJCPA head James Dunn

26. The two best collections on this subject are David Bromley and Anson Shupe, *The New Christian Politics* (Macon, Ga.: Mercer University Press, 1984), and Robert Liebman and Robert Wuthnow, *The New Christian Right* (New York: Aldine, 1983).

27. Even Richard Jackson refers to his resentment of the "Foy Valentine era" generation of leaders. Valentine's retirement was an unpleasant matter in which he was replaced by a more "moderate" bureaucrat, Larry Baker, who was virtually "hounded" from office to be replaced by Richard Land.

28. Though NCR leaders have hinted through the years that this separation need not be so

for being too liberal on other social issues. He was, it was rumored, "soft" on abortion. He denounced conservative political organizing in the churches.[29] He believed that "prayer in school" violated the separation of church and state.

Abortion was kept constantly before Southern Baptists as a key moral concern and was an axis on which the CLC as well as the potential BJCPA change turned, but "school prayer" was apparently the shibboleth that the coalition most wanted Dunn to say. Dunn, confident that the Convention would continue to sustain and fund him, seemed to enjoy defying the Convention's new leadership. Although the SBC provided the lion's share of support for the BJCPA, it was not its only source of funds. And, even if the Convention were to cut off its giving, individual churches and associations within the denomination could—and Dunn believed would—still support him.

Frequently throughout the 1980s, motions to censure either Dunn or the BJCPA would surface at annual meetings. Each time they would be refused by the messengers. Then, in 1986, the fundamentalist leaders opted for a new tactic. Dan Daniels moved at the Atlanta meeting that the Convention sever ties with the BJCPA. This motion, as all such serious matters, was referred, in this case to the Executive Committee.[30] This was a turning point and a moderate tactical mistake. Rather than sweeping the idea under the rug, this referral gave the people most friendly to the motion the power to decide. The Executive Committee was filled with those who supported the coalition—including Judge Pressler himself—and who would be more likely than the Convention as a whole to alter the denomination's historic ties. In September 1986 the Executive Committee appointed a study group, headed by Gary Young of Phoenix, to research the BJCPA issue. Paul Pressler was a member of the group.

In October 1986, just one month later, the group recommended reforms in the manner in which the Convention related to the BJCPA. First, the Public Affairs Committee (PAC), the Southern Baptist group that related to the BJCPA, would be expanded from fifteen to eighteen members, thus giving Southern Baptists more numerical representation on the Joint Committee. Second, the number of "at-large" members on the PAC would increase

broad. Indeed, any "Moral Majority" type of political activity requires more of a convergence of the two than traditional Southern Baptist practice would ever have sanctioned.

29. As he points out often, however, he also denounced Jesse Jackson's use of churches for political organizing.

30. Motions may also be referred to the institution they directly concern.

from five to twelve, with a corresponding decrease in the number of "ex officio" representatives; this took denominational employees out of power and made new appointments, by the coalition, possible. Finally, the PAC, previously doing little beyond working with the BJCPA, would now be empowered by the Convention to act on motions and resolutions from the Convention that the BJCPA either failed to act on or in some way opposed.

In the fall of 1986 the BJCPA agreed to these conditions. The following spring the Executive Committee accepted them, with Judge Pressler promising to oppose defunding of the BJCPA if the Convention accepted these changes. In St. Louis that June the Convention did just that.

But the issue was far from settled. In August 1987, just after the annual meeting, the new PAC balked at Young's version of the new arrangement. In their view, because they were responsible for representing the SBC on the BJCPA and for acting alone when they saw fit, it followed that the denomination's funds should come first to them, to be funneled appropriately to the BJCPA as circumstances dictated. If this was not the case, they insisted, how could they get funds to act independently when necessary? Everyone thought this question had been answered satisfactorily in St. Louis in June, but unfortunately there were two different views of what that answer had been.

Predictably, the Executive Committee formed another study group to look at the finances of the BJCPA and the PAC. This was too slow for the PAC, which voted 8 to 4 to sever ties with the BJCPA (showing decisively where the new strength on the PAC lay). It also voted to support the nomination of Robert Bork to the U.S. Supreme Court. The Executive Committee refused to act on the vote to sever, telling the two groups to "work it out." Then-President Adrian Rogers even supported the BJCPA when the PAC threatened to deny them space in the exhibit hall at the San Antonio annual meeting. The study group decided that the new arrangement neither required nor prohibited Cooperative Program money from going through the PAC to the BJCPA. For 1988, it was decided, the BJCPA would still be funded directly, but the PAC could comment on that funding at the Executive Committee meetings. The PAC would also have a budget, though it would be a fraction of the BJCPA's appropriation of approximately $400,000. The study group also affirmed the traditional Baptist refusal to support political candidates, but at Judge Pressler's request they deleted a similar prohibition against supporting "appointments." The PAC support of Judge Bork remained intact.

Because the Executive Committee, the PAC, and the BJCPA had not reached a suitable agreement, the issue did not come to the floor of the annual meeting in San Antonio in 1988. In February of 1989, however, the Executive Committee took decisive action that would be brought before the messengers in Las Vegas. It voted to disband the PAC and to form a new commission, the Religious Liberty Commission (RLC), which would be the Southern Baptist presence in Washington. This group would relate to the BJCPA on behalf of Southern Baptists and would receive all Cooperative Program funds designated for "religious liberty" issues. It would have its own trustees and its own employees and would fund all programs—including the BJCPA—concerning religious freedom that Southern Baptists chose to support. In short, this was to be the new Southern Baptist voice in Washington, and its connection to the "independent" BJCPA was simply one of its functions. Though discussion of the new commission at the Executive Committee meeting was tense, sometimes even bitter, there was little doubt that the matter had already been decided. Some conservatives, notably Richard Land and Darrell Robinson, tried to substitute a motion that would have given new funds and expanded Washington operations to the CLC. Moderates, feeling that the rug was being jerked out from under them, pleaded for a compromise that took their own interests into account. Though the related votes were at times closer than expected, the Executive Committee voted to recommend the new RLC. Because this was a new commission and a bylaws change, the Convention would have to approve it at two successive meetings. Las Vegas was about to become the first showdown to determine not only the people who held leadership posts within the denomination's institutions, but also the shape of the institutions themselves. The debate was moving beyond "who did the business" to "how business was done." This would in many ways measure both the extent of the coalition's influence and the relative pull of precedent and history, to which Baptists had always tenaciously held fast. If there were limits to the coalition's influence on grassroots messengers, they would probably be exposed in this vote.

Such a possibility was not lost on the fundamentalists. Long before Southern Baptists arrived in Las Vegas there were signs that some leaders of the coalition did not want trouble there. President Jerry Vines, already concerned that many Southern Baptists (especially fundamentalist ones) would not want to come to Las Vegas, asked that internal division be kept low-key so missionary efforts would not be jeopardized. Accordingly, he asked the Executive Committee to postpone the vote on the RLC until the 1990 meeting in New Orleans.

Many predicted that this vote to postpone would be close and that postponement would set off a heated debate. Nothing could have been less true.

Vines made his motion and pleaded for unity. Frank Ingraham, a moderate leader, praised Vines for his inclination to bring peace. Nothing more was said, and the motion passed unanimously. The RLC would not be an official test case in Las Vegas.

Cynical moderates suggested that Vines's move had been more pragmatic than peaceful, that he had made his move because he was afraid fundamentalists could not muster a majority in Las Vegas. Vines's wide margin of victory belies such beliefs.

At the same time, however, the coalition leaders may have realized that the motion might fail even with a fundamentalist majority present. It is impossible for a scholar to question Vines's motives—if he says his concern was evangelizing Las Vegas, who can say otherwise? But it is quite possible that he, and other leaders, recognized that the middle of the Convention— some of whom voted for them as presidential candidates but were not active in fundamentalist causes—would not support this institutional change. Substitute motions meant to reduce funding for the BJCPA failed by substantial margins in later votes.

In late 1989 the motion to create a new Religious Liberty Commission quietly disappeared. It would not come as a motion from the Executive Committee in New Orleans, but any new motion from the floor was always a possibility. A motion to cut BJCPA funding from $400,000 to $50,000 did come, and succeeded. In Atlanta in 1991 the BJCPA was defunded completely and its program responsibilities given to the CLC.

The votes in New Orleans and Atlanta represented a short and simple end to a long and complex story. The democratic squabbles disappeared because one of the parties simply did not show up: there were many fewer moderates in New Orleans than in years past, and virtually no moderate activists at the Atlanta meeting.

Indeed, in Atlanta there was a quiet return to civility. Few fundamentalists took the opportunity to bash the defeated moderates or to promote their own specific agendas. The great conservative center of the denomination seemed to rest quietly in place again.

Does this new quiet, alongside an accomplished change of leadership, signal the success or the failure of democratic mechanisms in the SBC? On the one hand, the loyal, minority opposition party was vanquished to the point of withdrawal—signaling an apparent failure of democratic polity. On the other hand, the democratic mechanisms instituted the will of the majority and restored denominational harmony in a relatively short period, approximately twelve years. "Democracy" is clearly a key concept, but it must be understood in the context of other kinds of authority in the SBC.

3

What Southern Baptists Have Meant by Democracy

Ambiguity Within Consensus: Democracy and Bureaucracy

The history of the Southern Baptist Convention is, in part, the story of the struggle between the denomination's congregational, independent roots and its need for efficient, bureaucratic control. Its focus is the continual interplay between increased organizational coordination and the demand for democratic voice.

This interplay has been regulated by a series of formal procedures—that is, by the development of polity—capable of guiding the dual demands for organizational efficiency and democratic governance. As its polity has adjusted to new events and new environmental constraints, the SBC has become "political" in its continual attempts to balance these dual demands in the many organizational forms of power and authority they take.

What are the principal forms of institutional, organizational, or individual power and authority that swirl around, within, and between the larger tensions present in the Convention? The answer to that question properly begins where previous work leaves off. In his *Authority and Power in the Free Church Tradition*, Paul Harrison details the problems, and potential problems, the American Baptist Churches face because of their polity. The root of the problem, according to Harrison, is that by granting its officials very little recognized authority—the authority officially rests in the hands of autonomous churches—the denomination has actually given them more, rather than less, organizational power. The denomination is effectively run by the handful of bureaucrats in important posts; at best, the only check on their power comes from those with the money and time to attend annual meetings—those usually already "inside" the denomination's established network. Thus the insistence on individual autonomy ultimately removes the power from the grassroots level and discourages change or dissent. When the associations of local churches have no true representative function they do not wield any influence. What remains is a cacophony of individual voices rather than a concert of organized opinion. Says Harrison:

> The Baptists may have been wise when they removed the bishops from their places; but when they also eliminated the ecclesiastical authority of their own associations the bishops returned in business suits to direct affairs from behind the curtain of center stage. Since their responsibilities are prodigious their presence is acknowledged. But paradoxically, their power is unrestricted because their authority is so limited. When Baptists recognize that authority is more than a grant to power and that it also defines and therefore limits the uses of power, they may sustain the proximate harmony which they are seeking.[1]

Harrison offers this solution: American Baptists must cede representative power and authority to their associations. There must be a voice that speaks for the many churches in a given association, a voice that is able to represent those churches in the national decision-making process. Conversely, the churches must subject themselves to these truly representative decisions. The denomination's bureaucracy must be staffed by people who have specific responsibilities and who do not make major decisions beyond the scope of their prescribed duties; these people must be answerable to those "elected" by the denomination's membership. In this way, a fair distribution can be established so that all voices are represented.

Such a solution is both simple and impossible. It is simple because it is so recognizable and so obvious. As Harrison says, everyone knows how to participate in a formal system of power; the informal system is run by those who can.[2] In so large a group as American Baptists, as in American society, a

---

1. Harrison, *Authority and Power*, p. 227.
2. See ibid., chap. 5, on formal and informal power.

"polis" or "city-state" type of democracy, where citizens all gather to discuss and then decide the issues, is unmanageable. Therefore, members of such groups must admit their practical limitations and develop representative structures that can more adequately express the opinions of the whole.

This solution is impossible, however, because it is so contrary to Baptist principles. Baptists are committed to the autonomy of the local church as a matter of biblical certainty.[3] While a more representative style of democracy seems fairer, and rings true to our own experiences as American citizens, it jeopardizes a type of freedom that most Baptists are unwilling to risk. Harrison correctly points out that such freedom is in one sense meaningless if it means that the "free" units (here the churches) have less rather than more group (here the denomination) power. What he does not address so well, however, is the fact that many Baptists believe that the group is ultimately less important. Therefore, it is better to risk group problems with power and its dispersal than to threaten local church autonomy. In theory, at least, the denomination is not ultimately important.

In practice the denomination is very important. Though American Baptists do not near the numbers of Southern Baptists, they are still a large group with substantial programs at the national level. "Cooperative" funds and their use are still a matter of great concern, especially for members who dissent from the denomination's current national programs and their emphases.

Such dissent, Harrison argues, should be a catalyst for a more representative system. Although he recognizes that the loss of ultimate autonomy would be a stumbling block for some, and that some would even leave the denomination, he contends that more dissidents might be likely to *stay* if they knew that their voices were being heard and that they had a genuine chance to effect change. That is, a representative system pays closer attention to dissent than an establishment that acts according to precedent and its own wishes. His admonition to American Baptists might have been most instructive for Southern Baptist moderates in the middle 1970s:

> One of the problems never adequately faced by the Baptists is the adequate institutionalization or legitimation of dissident groups

3. Noted Southern Baptist leader Hershel Hobbs called local church autonomy "the greatest Southern Baptist strength, and at the same time the greatest challenge" (*Baptist Press* release, May 27, 1988). Though the discussion here is of American Baptists, it is not unfair to say that Baptists are more committed to local church autonomy than they are even to democracy in their denomination, because their denomination is seen as an extension of their churches and not the other way around.

within the denominational structure. The fundamentalists are justifiably considered a threat to the stability of the denominational structure, but little is gained by pushing them aside and awaiting the day
when they shall gain sufficient power to reverse the procedure. In the
world of secular politics the rights of the opposition are preserved
through such institutions as the party system, minority rights, and
civil liberties. It is a strong indictment against the Baptists that they
have not discovered any means to permit their own minorities a voice
in the convention. In fact, by means of a representational system
which fails to represent a shamefully large sector of the denomination, the Baptists have made efforts to curtail all dissenting voices.
In part, the excuse has been rooted in an experience of recent decades with a vocal minority which is bent on destroying the values of
denominational organization. But it has been shown that in all prob-
ability, even if the fundamentalists were to gain control of the national organization, they would find it necessary to be obedient to
the organizational imperatives if they wished to remain in power.[4]

This indictment of American Baptists, written well before the beginning
of the coalition's efforts within the Southern Baptist Convention, proved
prophetic indeed. History records that the "establishment" did push fundamentalists aside until those fundamentalists gained "sufficient power to reverse the procedure."[5] The important question now is: What will the fundamentalists do with their organizational power, and what, if anything, will
the rest of the denomination do about the new changes at the top of the
denomination? Are the "reforms" Harrison recommended to American Baptists still available to Southern Baptists, or has the context for discussion
deteriorated to the point that there is nothing left to do but battle it out at
the ballot box?

It is unlikely that reforms such as Harrison's would ever be accepted wholeheartedly by Southern Baptists. Sullivan, an authority on Southern Baptist
polity, calls a system in which churches form associations, which combine
to form state conventions, which together make up the Southern Baptist
Convention, "totally unacceptable":

4. Harrison, *Authority and Power*, p. 223.
5. Both moderates and fundamentalists recognize this, producing the double effect of hard-
ening the attitude of fundamentalists toward moderates' claims of being treated unfairly, and
increasing moderates' guilt and frustration with the current turn of events.

> If our Southern Baptist denomination were constructed according to the prevailing misunderstanding [the organizational chain mentioned above], it would in time likely evolve into a totalitarian system illustrated by a pyramid-type organization—akin to the organization of a corporate structure. . . . All churches are at the top level; all other Baptist bodies are at a lower level in the denomination's organizational chart.[6]

Such a commitment to the principles of congregationalism would be difficult to alter. Local church autonomy and direct democracy in the local church, whatever their organizational risks, are simply part of what it is to be Baptist.[7] But there are other, practical, reasons that such a change in polity is unlikely. For many years the Southern Baptist establishment resisted change; indeed, the requirements for registering messengers at annual meetings, and dollar amounts in annual giving, are basically the same as they were in the late 1800s.[8] The new fundamentalist leadership is not apt to look favorably on recommendations for changing the polity to be more "fair" now that the situation is reversed. When a motion to change the "dollar limit," the minimum amount that must be contributed to the Cooperative Program per messenger, was brought before the Executive Committee it received a cool reception.

Eldon Miller, chair of the subcommittee under whose auspices the recommendation fell, commented that it was an odd coincidence that such a proposal was surfacing now after more than 100 years under the same system. He spoke against such a change, saying that it discriminated against the smaller churches and limited participation. "Participation," he said, "should always be encouraged. The more Baptists we get together, the better chance we have to come to a true understanding." To equate participation and cooperation too closely with dollar amounts would, in his view, be potentially harmful.[9]

6. James Sullivan, *Baptist Polity as I See It* (Nashville, Tenn.: Broadman Press, 1983), p. 44.

7. An excellent example of this commitment is the unwillingness of the Southern Baptist Alliance to adopt a more "presbyterian" representative structure at their 1988 meeting. Even these most liberal of Southern Baptists, who are also the most concerned about being disenfranchised, were unwilling to abandon their access to direct democracy.

8. As mentioned above, the stipulation that each church is allowed one messenger simply for "cooperating" and is given an additional messenger for every $250 in unrestricted giving to the convention's work—up to a total of ten messengers—was established in 1880.

9. From observation of the February 1989 meeting of the Executive Committee meeting in Nashville.

Thus the idea of joining together to reach consensus, always the Baptist ideal model, stands its ground against the challenges of "representative" models of polity. Because the congregational tradition is so strong, and because that tradition has been used as a weapon by both sides when they were in power, a shift to a more pure "representative" model such as Harrison recommended for American Baptists is unlikely for Southern Baptists.

Ambiguity Without Consensus: The Development of Procedural Polity

That does not mean that ideas such as fairness, justice, rights, and even equal representation have no role in Southern Baptist life. I believe that they do. Democracy, even if not Harrison's true representative type, plays a leading role in the denomination's polity. The task of this analysis is to establish just what that role is and to put it in context alongside the roles of charisma and bureaucracy. If we can understand the relationship of those three, and their relationship to the larger cultural context in which they were formed, then we can better answer the questions from the preceding chapter concerning *why* the Southern Baptist denomination finds itself where it does and *where* it is going.

The SBC has always considered itself democratic insofar as it never intended to establish a ruling body that could promulgate doctrines or direct funds by fiat. The ideal, from the first utterances of the organization in 1845, was a cooperative effort among independent churches who had similar beliefs and, especially, similar mission goals. Messengers from those churches were to meet every three years to determine the proper use of the denomination's pooled funds[10] and little else. The organization was intended to be guided, as a practical matter, from the bottom up.

It would be rash indeed to rush from such a statement to the conclusion that the SBC was intended to be the type of democracy we associate with western nations and states. There is little hint that the Convention was considered a forum for competing interests. As I have endeavored to point out, the denomination's founders envisioned a consensus model of polity. While it is true that the messengers would get together as equals to chart the

---

10. And even those funds were not "pooled" in any general way. For many years, Southern Baptists did all their giving by designating funds for particular enterprises.

Convention's course, it is only our liberal prejudice that might assume that they therefore expected to thrash out complex theological issues in an open forum. On the contrary, they expected to come together in a common understanding of God's will for their lives; their forum existed primarily to handle practical details, such as where the money was to be spent.

Such a polity emphasized all of the distinct principles of the Baptist heritage. The polity was congregational, emphasizing the autonomy both of the local church and of the individual believer. Southern Baptists, as Baptists everywhere and at all times, refused to use creedal statements to enforce doctrinal conformity, "preferring to rely upon the competency of a regenerate believer to interpret the Scriptures rightly under the guidance of the Holy Spirit."[11] Torbet places this principle "at the heart of Baptist democracy." Such a principle of autonomy for churches and individuals provides a rough spiritual equality, and some measure of equality—whether equal access to God's guidance, as in this case, or "one person, one vote"—is a necessary foundation for any democracy.

Historian George McDaniel describes a Baptist congregation as "a gospel church . . . an organized body of baptized believers equal in rank and privileges, administering its affairs under the headship of Christ, united in the belief of what he has taught, covenanting to do what he has commanded, and cooperating with other like bodies in Kingdom movements."[12] While this description emphasizes "equality," it must be remembered that it places "unity" on an equal footing. While Baptists have historically upheld individual autonomy in interpreting scripture—the priesthood of the believer—they have not necessarily expected or welcomed a plurality of interpretations.

If the sacred scriptures are, as Torbet has said, "the sole norm for faith and practice" in the Baptist tradition, then the interpretation of those scriptures takes on an enormous importance. It is all too easy for late twentieth-century readers to conclude that the mixture of the concepts "sola scriptura" and "individual autonomy in interpreting scripture" produced multiple theological views and multiple assessments of the importance of particular passages. There is little evidence, however, that early Southern Baptists entertained this possibility or that they considered it a major problem.

Indeed, the concept of "priesthood of the believer" and the individual interpretation of scripture it required was grounded in the faith that the

---

11. Torbet, *History of the Baptists*, p. 24.
12. George McDaniel, *The Churches of the New Testament* (New York: Richard Smith, 1921), p. 23.

Bible was easily read by everyone and was plain to understand.[13] Southern Baptists expected, and received, an overwhelming consensus on what Christ had commanded them to do: preach the gospel to a lost world. The disputes would be over practical methods for carrying out that command.[14] If scripture's meaning had been obscured for some by human intrusions, God's word was still clear and unequivocal enough for most Southern Baptists.

But the possibility of such human intrusions was not to be taken lightly. Growing out of the Baptist belief in the authority of scripture and the autonomy of the individual and the local congregation was a firm commitment to religious liberty, best expressed in the separation of church and state. If Baptists were to be free, as churches and as individuals, to live by scripture's commands, they must be beyond the reach of civil interference. Many commentators go so far as to credit the exclusion of any religious tests in the U.S. Constitution to the tenacity and perseverance of the eighteenth-century Baptists in America. Southern Baptists were steeped in this tradition of church-state separation and fully expected to pursue their interests without external hindrance.

Southern Baptists are thus firmly rooted in the historic Baptist principles of autonomy, liberty, and the authority of scripture.[15] Although it would be wrong to claim that the Southern Baptist Convention was formed specifically to foster these principles—it was in fact formed to do mission work cooperatively in an environment in which slaveholders could be missionaries—it would be equally wrong to discard the Convention's commitment to them. They do not surface frequently in the earliest Southern Baptist literature because they were simply taken for granted. The new Convention was

13. The extent to which this view was grounded in Scottish "common sense" philosophy, and the degree to which this early modern worldview is still held by fundamentalists, is a matter to which I shall return. See Marsden, *Fundamentalism and American Culture.*

14. A critical mind might well ask: "If the scripture is so plain, why are there so many different denominations? Why even is there an end to cooperation between northern and southern Baptists?" The first answer a Southern Baptist might give, though it grates liberal sensibilities, is that other denominations have bastardized the scriptures with human, social influences. The second answer is similar: northern Baptists have allowed a cultural influence that is suprascriptural—namely, slavery—to influence their thinking. While both responses might seem to belie the fact that they themselves are culturally determined, coming out of a reading of scripture that is itself culture-bound, we must remember that mid-nineteenth-century Christians had no such "critical" perspective. Also, we do well to remember H. R. Niebuhr's admonition in his *Social Sources of Denominationalism* (New York: Henry Holt & Co., 1929) that there is in fact *a* message in scripture that we must unfortunately endeavor to live out in our finite, human forms, which are *always* socially determined.

15. From Torbet, *A History of the Baptists*, who adds a fourth: "baptism of believers." Though I have no argument with including such a principle, it is simply not relevant to the discussion at hand.

about cooperative missions; that people who subscribed to these principles were the ones to do that mission work was beyond question.

The move to cease cooperation with other, northern Baptists was itself a move toward greater independence. Johnson's original proposal for this co-operative enterprise, while focusing on the significance of this "judicious concentration" of efforts, still pledges "perfect liberty" to each contributor in "specifying the object or objects to which his amount shall be applied, as he please. . . ."[16] Southern Baptists wished at once to stress their freedom and their strength in association. This was, as Sullivan pointed out, a body with the local church at the top and all other entities further down the organizational chart.

Thus the SBC was democratic, but in a distinctly populist way. It styled itself as a cooperative effort among free equals, an effort emphasizing both the liberty of the churches it comprised and the liberty of the whole from the civil authorities. Its decisions would be made by messengers from the cooperating bodies and not by appointees or official representatives. Its authority rested ostensibly not in ecclesiastical leadership or in representative government but in the plain instruction of the Bible. In all of these ways, the SBC was a populist form of democracy.

The SBC and Its Environment: Similarities and Differences

If the SBC was a democratic organization of sorts, so too was the nation of which it was a part. And if "democracy" could be applied both to the SBC and to mid-nineteenth-century America, then the term's descriptive ability is seriously in doubt. On the brink of a catastrophic civil war, America had become an archetypal forum for "competing interests." Was the nation's infrastructure ultimately to be based on agriculture or on industry? Was the final authority to rest with states or with the federal government? These issues were at the heart of perhaps the most crucial (and unresolvable) debate about America's future, a debate finally settled more on the battlefield than at the ballot box.

If this contention between two (or more) visions of the right constituted a democratic polity, then it would seem that the SBC's polity must surely be

16. Baker, *Baptist Source Book*, p. 114.

described differently. But perhaps not so differently. Both American and SBC polities sought to promote a general equality in participation. Both promoted liberty for individuals and for their voluntarily chosen organizations. Both, at least in their original manifestations, had sought a limited role for the "central" organization and a wide dispersal of power.

The apparent differences might best be described not as differences in *form* but as differences in *content* and *level of organizational maturity*. While the basic structure of the polity may have been similar—equality, voting, limited central control—the people who lived *within* the two structures were quite different, and the structures themselves were at much different stages of development.

The first claim, that the membership of each polity was different, is the easier to establish. As I have said, in the mid-1800s America was a country divided. It was not only a melting pot, comprising a variety of different cultural and ethnic backgrounds, but also a battleground (first figuratively and then literally) on which the wars over industrialization and the role of technology were being waged. There was no clear vision of the "American way of life," but instead deep disagreement over the nation's future. The ballot box was, until the controversy reached its breaking point, the established forum for public debate. In such a large and disparate society, however, such a forum was insufficient. The commitment to democracy itself meant different things to different people. Without analyzing the myriad causes of the Civil War, one can still note the oft-rehearsed differences between southern agrarianism and northern industrialization, which were coupled with the different democratic perspectives of federalism and "states rights."

Although the point is easily and often overstated, the South was much more homogeneous than the nation as a whole. As Samuel Hill has so well documented, the South was properly called "the Solid South" because there was a genuine, palpable cultural solidarity. Moreover, this solidarity had religion as the "conservator and reinforcer of, as distinct from agent for change within, popular (white) southern culture."[17] The dominant form of this religion was Evangelical Protestantism, a form itself dominated by Baptists.[18]

17. Samuel Hill et al., *Religion and the Solid South* (New York: Abingdon Press, 1972), p. 22.

18. Hill (ibid.) notes the irony in the fact that evangelicalism, itself concerned with "change," should be the basis for conservatism. It is worth noting here that the difference may well be between "individual" change and "social" change. While "winning souls" and personal piety are strong southern concerns, the sort of evangelicalism associated with the "social gospel" never had the same impact in the South among whites.

We could expect the membership within the new Southern Baptist de-mocracy—the structure's "contents," if you will—to be similarly homoge-neous. Religion was not simply a practice or a facet of one's life, but the vehicle by which culture, in Geertz's terms, was transmitted. It was the car-rier of those "historically transmitted patterns of meanings embodied in sym-bols, a system of inherited conceptions expressed in symbolic forms by means of which men communicate, perpetuate and develop their knowledge and attitudes about life."[19] It would be an overstatement to claim that "to be southern was to be Baptist." But the nearly tautological claim—"to be Southern Baptist was to be southern" was surely true—and not as trivial as it first appears. To be Southern Baptist was to be southern in political, moral, religious, and cultural identity, not just as a geographical reference. Southern Baptists represented a "culture" in a manner which those more familiar with other American denominations often find difficult to under-stand.[20]

It is therefore no surprise that the framers of the early SBC did not expect their democratic organization to function like their country. They expected popular consensus. And the reason they might consciously have given for that expectation—"that God's word is always and everywhere the same to all people"—is even more compelling in a society in which there is not likely to be great division over understanding or interpretation. Democracy in an homogeneous environment is much different from democracy in a hetero-geneous one, but it is democracy nonetheless.

Difference in *content* was not, however, the only reason for the differences between the democracy of the nation and that of the Southern Baptist Con-vention. The American polity was now well into its first century and had adjusted many times to deal with its changing environment. Although the federal government in no way approached the imposing size or scope it enjoys today, it had already moved well beyond the very limited role it played in the eighteenth century. A significant bureaucracy, although paltry by late twentieth-century standards, was already in place.[21] The nation itself was

19. Clifford Geertz, "Religion as a Cultural System," in his *Interpretation of Cultures* (New York: Basic Books, 1973).

20. As H. R. Niebuhr pointed out in his *Social Sources of Denominationalism*, American denominations have historically all been segregated along lines of class, color, and social status. I am claiming here that the SBC, as *the* religious mainstay in Hill's "solid South," went beyond even Niebuhr's distinction. It was not a denomination caused by culture, but rather part and parcel of its culture.

21. This bureaucracy proved to be merely the groundwork for a bureaucratic revolution that would enable America to move from a crumbling system of autonomous communities to an

expanding; James K. Polk, whose expansionist supporters adopted the cry "Fifty-Four Forty or Fight," was inaugurated as President in 1845 amid a flurry of westward movement. America was a growing and changing nation, and her federal political structures were growing and changing with it.

By contrast, the nascent SBC had little or no central authority. Following the well-established pattern of doing mission work through societies, the SBC merely sought to create one general convention that would be responsible for the various mission efforts. As detailed in Chapters 1 and 2, the societies were still independent operations to which contributors could give or not give, at their own discretion. In W. B. Johnson's words, each contributor had "perfect liberty" to designate the recipient of "his" gifts. [22]

That the SBC would develop into an organization with a strong central authority and an enormous budget comprising primarily undesignated, cooperative funds, much as America had as a nation, speaks volumes about the powers of rationalization and bureaucracy. It also suggests, although it does not demonstrate, that the apparent differences between "consensus" and "competing interest" models of democracy may be better described as different stages in the model's development rather than as two completely different models.

Suggesting that the SBC's democratic polity differed from that of the nation more in content and maturity than in form or substance does not, however, lift the responsibility for pointing out the most striking difference between the two. The nation was committed to freedom and equality on the basis of reason; America's guiding principles were truths "held to be self-evident." The nation's founders were deists, holding very high views of the regularity and predictability of nature and of nature's laws. [23] Freedom of conscience, ownership of property, and freedom of speech were all considered part of what it was to be human. [24]

The SBC, on the other hand, was committed ultimately to a spiritual purpose. In W. B. Johnson's address to the public, he said that the Conventions' principles were "conservative," while "also, as we trust, equitable and liberal." But the objects of the convention are "the extension of the Mes-

---

organization built on structural hierarchy in the early twentieth century. See Robert Wiebe, *The Search for Order, 1877–1920* (New York: Hill & Wang, 1967).

22. Women within the nascent SBC were both fund-raisers and major contributors, as they have been throughout the denomination's history.

23. Adam Smith's *Wealth of Nations,* published fortuitously in 1776, is perhaps the most eloquent statement of faith in the beneficence of the laws of nature and the social intercourse between "men."

24. At least what it was to be a white, male human.

siah's kingdom, and the glory of our God. Not disunion with any of his people; not the upholding of any form of human policy, or civil rights; but God's glory, and Messiah's increasing reign."[25] The SBC had a polity shaped by equality, freedom, and universal participation; however, that polity was always in service of spiritual ends.

The original constitution of the SBC does not contain any references to God or to scripture. As a practical matter, this new democratic organization had a shape similar to civil organizations. But the Convention, it must always be remembered, was not formed finally to protect rights[26] or property, as a civil government might be, but to advance missionary goals that were themselves rooted in a biblical view of the world. The authority of scripture was thus destined to play a role for which there is no neat civil parallel.

Despite these differences—pluralism versus homogeneity, expanded central organization versus a very limited one, natural and rational foundations versus spiritual and biblical ends—it should be clear that the SBC was created as an "American" organization. Its members may have had as their object "God's glory, and Messiah's increasing reign" but they were convinced that in the promotion of these they could find, in Johnson's words, "no necessity for relinquishing any of our civil rights." Johnson continued: "We will never interfere with what is Caesar's. We will not compromit what is God's."[27]

The fact that the Convention's principles were democratic and liberal was not all that important in the early years. As documented earlier, there was no central organization to speak of, each mission work or benevolence operating as an independent society. In addition, the membership was so likeminded on many things that "rights" within the Convention, thought of as the claim of one person or group over against another, needed little protection. The importance of the democratic mechanisms built into the polity would not be evident until the convention became less homogeneous and began to develop a more permanent central organization.

This development—highlighted by the establishment of the Executive Committee, the growth of the Sunday School Board, and the introduction of the Cooperative Program—tested the polity's ability to handle dissent and change. The results were not always positive. Even the Convention's earliest, decentralized societies were met with suspicion. Many Baptists preferred to

25. Baker, *Baptist Source Book*, pp. 120–21.
26. Rights were part of the picture. Southern Baptists felt that their civil rights were being denied by their northern brethren when slaveholders were denied missionary status.
27. Baker, *Baptist Source Book*, p. 121.

do mission work through their local churches and associations or state organizations. At several points it looked as though the new Convention would
divide into many smaller groups. The localism and populism associated with
the Landmark movement were widely influential even among those who were
not "Landmarkers." The fear of bureaucracy and of a loss of local autonomy
dogged every attempt to centralize, consolidate, or expand.

But expand the Convention did, sometimes almost in spite of itself.[28]
Much like the nation in which it was formed, the denomination expanded
westward (and also eventually northward). Its strong sphere of influence
moved beyond the "solid" southeast to the southern plains and the desert
southwest, especially Arkansas, Oklahoma, Texas, and Arizona. The eventual push to the west coast brought Southern Baptist influence, including
even a seminary, to California.[29]

Also like the nation itself, the SBC began in the early 1900s to develop
an ever more specialized bureaucracy capable of identifying and performing
specific functions.[30] The Home Mission Board, the Foreign Mission Board,
and the Sunday School Board each created smaller, specialized programs
responsible for ever more specialized tasks.[31] In addition, the denomination

28. A popular and a plausible view among Southern Baptists is that controversy results in
ever-greater evangelism and thus growth. Said James Baker of the current controversy, "Only
one thing is certain; both sides will continue to grow. Baptists, like cats, multiply by fighting"
(Christian Century, March 5, 1980, pp. 254–57).

29. Baker (SBC, p. 340) notes that the center of the denomination moved west primarily
in the period from 1877 to 1917.

30. Wiebe argues that such "bureaucratization" was the result of a loss of personal, informal
community. It was, he says, "derived from the regulative, hierarchical needs of urban-industrial
life. Through rules with impersonal sanctions, it sought continuity and predictability in a
world of endless change. It assigned far greater power to government—in particular, to a variety of flexible administrative devices—and encouraged the centralization of authority" (Wiebe,
Search for Order, preface, p. xiv). Ben Primer follows this argument in contending that the
centralized, bureaucratic structure became the form for American churches, beginning in the
early twentieth century (Ben Primer, The Bureaucratization of the Church: Protestant Response to
Modern, Large-Scale Organization, 1876–1929 [Ph.D. diss., Johns Hopkins University, 1977]).

31. Before its reorganization in 1988 (which made it an even more "vertical" hierarchy),
the Home Mission Board had "sections" for Evangelism, Missions, Planning, and Services,
with vice-presidents over them. Under each of these sections are "divisions." The Missions
Section alone has the Associational Missions Division, the Metropolitan Missions Division,
the Chaplaincy Division, the Church Extension Division, the Church Loans Division, the
Language Services Division, and the Missions Ministry Division. Each division is run by a
director and has "departments." The Missions Ministry Division alone has the Black Church
Relations Department, the Church and Community Ministries Department, the Christian
Social Ministries Department, the Interfaith Witness Department, and the Special Missions

created commissions and standing committees to handle matters that did not fall directly under the purview of its boards.

This bureaucratic growth did not happen overnight. The Convention did not awake one morning to find that its independent, grassroots membership had been enslaved by a powerful outside force. However, the fact that such an enormous organization could develop in a little more than 100 years,[32] during which time the nation was committing so many of her resources to one civil war and two world wars, is still remarkable. Lacking both the institutional base of more-established denominations in the mid-1800s, and the benefit of an influx of immigrants who were already Southern Baptists (such as the one enjoyed by the Roman Catholic church, which went quickly from one of the smaller organized religious groups in America to the largest) the SBC became in those hundred or so years the largest Protestant denomination in the United States.

If the Convention could be likened to the nation in its development of a specialized bureaucracy and in its geographic expansion, so too was its development of a centralized, more general authority familiar. Although Americans have reopened the national debate about the relative size of the roles played by national, state, and local authorities, it is no longer debatable that ultimate political power rests in Washington. Even though there are thousands of state and city executives, legislative bodies, and judicial circuits, there can be no doubt that final authority belongs to the President, the Congress, and the Supreme Court. The growth of bureaucratic specialization has meant a stronger, not weaker, center.[33]

The line of SBC organizational growth runs roughly parallel. The development of the Cooperative Program (CP) in the 1920s, built on undesignated gifts, meant that some central authority would make allocations and set priorities. Though this responsibility was intended, and still is, to be handled by the messengers at the annual meetings, the size and range of the Convention made this a practical impossibility from the program's inception. The nuts-and-bolts running of the Convention had to be done by the

---

Ministry Department, each of which has directors and associate directors and assistant directors (the Special Missions Ministry Department of the Missions Ministry Division of the Missions Section has six of these), with research and clerical staffs too.

32. Though the denomination is now nearing its 150th birthday, most of the bureaucracy was in place by the 1950s.

33. See Wiebe, *Search for Order*. See also Clinton Rossiter, *The American Presidency* (New York: Harcourt Brace, 1956), who argues that the power of the American presidency has grown, not receded, during the years of rapid bureaucratic growth.

elected Executive Committee, created less than a decade before the Cooperative Program, and the appointed, paid denominational executives. Though the executives and trustees of each separate organization—board, commission, seminary, etc.—were and are very important and largely independent in running their own programs, much of their direction and their money come through the Executive Committee acting on behalf of the Convention. The Convention sets guidelines and a general direction for the denomination. Following those directions is left to the central authorities in Nashville, who in turn leave the details to the relevant agencies involved.[34]

The development of such an order in the SBC should not be particularly surprising. The Convention's growth made small programs run by independent and autonomous agencies impossible for several reasons. First and foremost, the denomination's constituency was broadening. Baptists on the "frontier" in Abilene did not have the same mission needs as those in Charleston or Richmond. The boards required specialized programs tailored to the needs of particular groups or areas.

Second, the denomination was growing numerically and geographically. It was no longer possible reasonably to expect that the messengers could handle all of the daily decision-making responsibilities such a large organization required. Furthermore, it became increasingly difficult to manage such a large organization on donations by churches that specifically designated what the donations were to be used for but that had little knowledge of the denomination's immediate needs. Creation of the Executive Committee and the Cooperative Program, along with the specialization of the agencies, were pragmatic responses to a changing environment.

Third, the Convention's "solidity" was under increasing pressure. The "new" Southern Baptists in New Mexico were not necessarily part of the "solid" southern culture of Georgia, Alabama, Tennessee, and the Carolinas. Indeed, even the Southern Baptists in those core states were becoming more diverse. The "new South" that emerged after the Civil War became more industrial, turning to steel and textiles, and thus more urban. Although agriculture was still a staple of the area's economy, the image of a rural, agrarian region was quickly fading. Southern Baptists, particularly in cities, turned to an increasingly educated clergy.[35]

34. This mirrors the national political scene, where individuals do not usually vote on referendums or policies, but on representatives who will be responsive to "the public will." The difficulty in determining just what that "public will" is, and the rampant disagreements over it, is predictably similar too.

35. Baker (SBC, pp. 331ff.) notes that this move was already under way in the South even before 1845. He cites reaction against Campbellism as one possible cause, but attributes the

During these changes the SBC began to develop a new, "heightened denominational consciousness." Intertwined with all of the factors we normally associate with modernization—increasing pluralism, the advance of industry and technology, education, and the wide dissemination of ideas—was a "definite movement toward group promotion of benevolences common to all Southern Baptists." The states began to develop uniform denominational emphases and to standardize statistical reports on progress. Authority in state conventions came increasingly under the control of the executive secretaries, with several states developing cooperative and even consolidated structures. Use of a "national" curriculum produced by the Sunday School Board grew. Perhaps most tellingly, the image of outstanding minister began to shift from the eloquent orator to the loyal denominational leader.[36]

It is interesting to note the seeming paradox in this development. As the denomination grew larger and more diverse, it developed an increasingly *uniform* organizational structure. In a similar fashion, as the bureaucracy grew in scope and became more specialized, it developed a stronger base of *central* control. In short, as the denomination broadened it did not seem to become more disconnected and unpredictable, but more *regular*. It developed rational, fixed structures to deal with its changing and expanding environment.

The SBC thus followed the pattern common to most ongoing institutions, first noted by Max Weber. The power vested in charismatic individuals—the great preachers—drifted gradually into the hands of the great organizers; power became more a matter of office than of person.[37] Methods for dealing with a changing environment were rationalized: they became regular and predictable, shaped by the forces that maximized results. In short, the gradual changes that began just after the Civil War, as noted above, introduced the possibility of a large and expanding bureaucracy governed by *rules* and *standards*.

---

change primarily to a rise in the general level of education. Although Baker's assertion of this rise is difficult to corroborate for this date, it does seem likely that large cities now had two or three educated pastors where before there might have been only one. For further elucidation of this argument, see also Ammerman, *Baptist Battles*, esp. chap. 5.

36. This section, and the quotations, are taken directly from Baker, *SBC*, pp. 335ff.

37. Said Weber: "With these routinizations, rules in some form always come to govern. The prince or the hierocrat no longer rules by virtue of purely personal qualities, but by virtue of acquired or inherited qualities, or because he has been legitimized by an act of charismatic election" (from "The Social Psychology of the World Religions," in *From Max Weber: Essays in Sociology*, ed. H. H. Geerth and C. Wright Mills [New York: Oxford University Press, 1946], p. 297).

By the middle of the twentieth century the SBC was truly an enormous organization responsible for thousands of specific tasks. As such, it seemed at times to mirror its surrounding culture. In the aftermath of the Great Depression the national government had grown from the small, slowly consolidating federal power established in the wake of the Civil War into a bureaucratic organization of unprecedented scope. An economy that not so long ago was largely agrarian was now primarily industrial; moreover, great advancements in technology and communications were already sowing the seeds for the transition from a blue-collar to a white-collar labor market. America was, in many ways, a society dominated by the influence and guidance of large-scale bureaucracies.[38] The movement of the SBC in this direction made sense in terms of its environment.

It made sense to much of its membership as well. The increasingly educated clergy was well aware of the benefits of organization.[39] And lay members, moving with the rest of the South (and indeed the rest of the nation) into a more urban and suburban middle-class, were accustomed to participating through committees and layers of management.[40] Further, they were accustomed to expressing their views through democratic procedures. These were the norms both in society and in their churches and annual meetings.[41] Their new success was premised on an orderly, rational world that functioned according to established rules.

38. C. Wright Mills describes the situation somewhat bleakly: "In all this bureaucratic usurpation of freedom and of rationality, the white-collar people are the interchangeable parts of the big chains of authority that bind the society together" (*White Collar: The American Middle Classes* [New York: Oxford University Press, 1951], introduction, p. xvii). While Mills is correct to identify the white-collar middle class as the "stuff" of American society, he surely overshoots when he says: "There is no plan of life. Among white-collar people, the malaise is deeply rooted; for the absence of any order of belief has left them morally defenseless as individuals and politically impotent as a group." Mills's obsession with class interests caused him to miss the many other spheres in which such people might express themselves both individually and corporately.

39. Ammerman's data put the level of Southern Baptist clergy with a B.A. or beyond at 78 percent ("Mobilizing the Messengers," paper presented at the Southern Baptist Research Association, June 7, 1986, p. 5).

40. Ammerman (ibid.) notes that 44 percent of Southern Baptists regard themselves as better off than their parents and that more than half are in white-collar jobs. A substantial majority are in the $20,000–$50,000 salary range, with $20,000–$35,000 the single largest group (41 percent).

41. The Center for Religious Research found that an overwhelming number of Baptists (more than 80 percent) either disagreed or strongly disagreed with the statement that "pastors should have the final authority in the local church." In their written responses to questions about church authority, moderates were especially likely to promote the idea of church democracy and to downplay pastoral control.

Such a claim should not be used to characterize unfairly these middle-class participants as automatons, cogs in some giant maze of overlapping systems. If the systems ran according to established rules, rule number one was that the participants were *free* to choose their level of participation. Furthermore, they were committed to the notion that the system must be *fair*, rewarding effort and ingenuity. That there were rational rules was more often seen as a liberating, not constraining, fact of life. The American dream was that the rules kept privilege in check, making the playing field more level for everyone.[42]

But in the SBC, as elsewhere, some were more equal than others. While increases in the general level of education and the expectation of democratic participation worked to decrease the distance between clergy and laity—Baptists have historically downplayed the distinction between them—bureaucracy and democracy were undoubtedly viewed differently by the two groups. Some pastors were comfortable assuming "management" roles; others resented it. Just what "priesthood of the believer," a traditional Baptist prerogative, and "soul competency" in the interpretation of scripture would mean in this new organizational structure remained to be seen.

Furthermore, there was a sense in which "democracy" and "freedom" rang more true to the experiences of laypeople in the church. For them, the church was truly a voluntary organization, one among many in their lives; if they disagreed substantially with current policy, they could vote with their feet. Clergy were likely to be more connected, in substance as well as in organizational theory, to the bureaucracy and to the denomination as a whole. They could leave, of course, but most of the organizational resources they enjoyed—annuities, literature, educational centers, and so on—were operated through the denomination.

This distinction between clergy and laity notwithstanding, the growth of bureaucracy in the SBC and the standardization of programs rang true to the other social experiences of its membership. They were free in their local churches, as in their homes, to choose as they pleased. To participate in the affairs of the larger world, however, they needed to deal through large orga-

42. Though it is not the place of this research to substantiate such a claim, it is plausible to suggest that both World War II and the civil rights movement point up the high value placed on freedom and fairness. White middle-class Americans were willing to sacrifice on behalf of others, in the case of World War II, and to give up a measure of their favored social status, in the case of the civil rights movement—*because* they were heavily invested in a growing bureaucratic "system" of government and corporations, not in spite of that fact. They were so committed to freedom and fairness that they had no choice but to act as they did, even when it might not have seemed to be in their immediate self-interest.

nizations capable of assimilating and processing all the necessary information. Most mid-twentieth-century Americans would not expect to designate where their money would be best spent; they recognized the world as a large place, its needs beyond the comprehension of any single individual or small group. Gradually shifting the responsibility for managing such affairs and for overseeing the direction of mass participation to a large bureaucracy was very much "the way of the world," a fact not lost on those who still considered the world a hostile place.

4

Scriptural Law and the Rise of Fundamentalism

The Fundamentalist Coalition's Heritage

The "benefits" of education and urbanization, along with technological advance and the rise of bureaucratic organization, were neither universally enjoyed nor necessarily regarded as beneficial. If a wide segment of the American population, including a corresponding chunk of Southern Baptists, were heavily invested in the liberal virtues of a pluralistic society based on rational organization, there were still many for whom this "advance" of culture was highly suspect. The emergent bureaucracy in the SBC had its roots in the idea of democratic cooperation that characterized the Convention's founding. It was, in many ways, the logical extension into twentieth-century America of the "judicious concentration" Johnson had proposed. But there were other important ideas in the Convention's past—especially the priority of the local church and ultimate biblical authority—that had not been so neatly rationalized or institutionalized. The Convention's earliest discontents may have been submerged as the denomination grew and prospered, but they had not disappeared.

Indeed, the hostility the Landmarkers felt toward central planning and organization gave way to an open contempt for bureaucracy, or any form of external authority, in the fundamentalist movements of the 1920s. And if the shouts of these critics were muted by the rapid numerical and geographical advance of the denomination through the middle of the century, their resentment remained. The Elliott controversy in the early 1960s signaled a new era of resistance from those who were discontented with the denomination's development. The denomination's leadership was called to account for programs and literature that did not represent the conservative, including fundamentalist, biblical views of many of their constituents.

As detailed earlier, the biblical conservatives "won" the convention votes both on the Elliott controversy and on the second Genesis controversy in the early 1970s. They succeeded, over time, in having Elliott dismissed and the offending books removed from circulation within the denomination. They did not, however, make any permanent organizational changes. The Sunday School Board never truly "recanted" its decision to print the Davies and Honeycutt volumes, or its failure to carry out the Convention's wishes in their first revision. Moreover, Honeycutt went on to become president of Southern Seminary, an office of great prestige and considerable influence within the denomination. Thus these victories at the annual meeting did little to soothe the resentment and mistrust a substantial number of Southern Baptists still felt.

As with the American Baptist Churches, the SBC failed to include the fundamentalists in the bureaucratic leadership of the Convention. As Harrison noted concerning the American Baptist Convention, the SBC continued to push the fundamentalists aside, "awaiting the day when they [would] gain sufficient power to reverse the procedure." There was nothing built into the Convention's consensus model of democracy, or into the structure of its bureaucratic organization, which guaranteed legitimation to dissident voices. The organization was primarily structured around the goodwill of its leaders and a general agreement—one might even call it a gentleman's agreement—on the procedures that determined the denomination's direction. When the consensus failed and the goodwill soured, there was little left to compel the actors involved to behave as gentlemen.

The fundamentalists did gain sufficient power—at least a sufficient number of votes at the annual meetings—to begin "reversing the procedure" in 1979. And reverse it they did. Where there had been, in their opinion, no biblical conservatives on boards or committees, there were soon only biblical conservatives.[1] Although members of the denominational establishment still

1. To fundamentalists, "biblical conservatives" are fundamentalists. There can be no doubt that, by the general standards of demographers such as Gallup, a large majority of the SBC is biblically conservative, but the strictest inerrantists use a different yardstick.

had jobs—many were permanent, salaried employees or had appointments with specific tenures—most new appointments or hirings followed a strict fundamentalist line. The former establishment was now being pushed aside and had no choice but to try to regroup in order to challenge the new "establishment." Later, many simply gave up the fight and began planning a distinct though perhaps not completely separate group.

It is easy enough to see from this example that the process of rationalization and bureaucratization, indeed of secularization, does not flow as fluidly as its more sanguine proponents might have us believe. The Convention certainly developed rational structures—primarily democratic and bureaucratic ones—for dealing with its changing environment. The forces of modernization—insofar as they involve education, urbanization (or cosmopolitanization), and the advance of technology—were at work here as elsewhere. All of this was compatible with a well-defined tradition of cooperation. But there were other forces operating in the SBC that did not fit this modernizing pattern, at least at first blush. Understanding these forces, and the people who embody them, requires some understanding of the other traditions in the SBC, especially those associated with fundamentalism.

The most salient of these traditions is the reliance on biblical authority. From a larger perspective, nearly all Southern Baptists may appear to be biblical conservatives who rely heavily on biblical authority. To one another, though, Baptists often look widely diverse. To the nonbeliever, or even the non-Southern Baptist, agreement on the deity and the substitutionary atonement of Christ may look substantial; to those for whom these are a given, disagreement on virgin birth, a literal reading of the creation story, or even the reliability of Mosaic authorship assume a mantle of serious distinction. To understand the controversy in the SBC, one must understand the tradition of biblical authority and its role in the fundamentalist movement, represented by the Pressler-Patterson coalition.

However else they might be defined, fundamentalists are biblical literalists in a very strict sense. They believe in a literal, bodily creation of Adam and Eve and in a literal apocalypse found in a cryptic reading of the Revelation to Saint John.[2] They believe that the Bible contains *no errors* in matters of historic or scientific fact or in matters of faith or theology. Although the

2. While there is still wide agreement on the premillennial nature of that revelation, increased fundamentalist activities in the realm of social action threaten to undermine this emphasis. There is no threat, however, to the insistence on "literalism." Convention President Jerry Vines regularly details his belief in a literal resurrection, a literal second coming, and a literal heaven and hell.

term "inerrancy" seems to take on a technical sense in discussions of biblical authority, the basic fundamentalist position is simple enough. "Inerrant" means no errors, including no "mistaken" interpretations based on the cultural circumstances of the authors or advances in available information. Fundamentalism may be a complex topic, but at least from the perspective of its proponents its bottom line is plain.

Such "inerrancy" can be applied to most Southern Baptists, as well as to many other American Christians. By itself, strong reliance on scriptural authority does not adequately separate the fundamentalists we would associate with the Pressler-Patterson coalition in the SBC, or the Moral Majoritarians we associate with Jerry Falwell, from a host of other biblical conservatives. It is therefore necessary to say more about the specific character of fundamentalism as it goes beyond "mere" assertion of absolute biblical infallibility.[3]

Other key features of fundamentalism as an identifiable position include evangelism, separatism, and premillennialism.[4] If it is no longer the case that *all* fundamentalists hold the view that Christ will return in the rapture to take believers with him *before* the great tribulation and the thousand-year reign (the millennium) of Christ on earth, it is clear enough that most fundamentalists do think so. An inerrant view of scripture is historically intertwined with a dispensational view of history, and the dominant form of that dispensationalism expects Christ's return *before* the many events associated with the end of time.[5]

Predictably, it has been *post*millennialists—who believe that human effort and God's grace will bring about the thousand-year reign—who have been

3. As I have said, Ammerman refers to politically active, Moral Majoritarian types as "big F" Fundamentalists, and to others who share those inerrant biblical views but lack the other characteristics as "small f" fundamentalists. Although members of the SBC's coalition, notably Pressler, want to be known only as "biblical conservatives" (which they certainly are), I identify them as "fundamentalists" in order to separate them from other biblical conservatives who do not share their political or organizational interests.

4. Nancy Ammerman, "North American Protestant Fundamentalism," in *Fundamentalisms Observed*, ed. Martin E. Marty and R. Scott Appleby (Chicago: University of Chicago Press, 1990), pp. 4–8. Because there is no need, in my study, to go on at length about fundamentalism beyond its specific occurrence in the SBC, I have borrowed these defining characteristics from this clear and concise exposition.

5. Dispensationalism is a theory that breaks all of human history into different epochs, or dispensations, each having its own peculiar form of relationship between God and humans. One source of the enormous importance placed on the authority of scripture comes from the fact that in this age (the church age), unlike dispensations when God and humans spoke more directly, revelation comes primarily from the written texts. While not all fundamentalists downplay direct revelation or "prophecy" to the same degree, the high view of scripture relative to these other forms of divine inspiration is worth noting.

most closely associated with social activism. Premillennialists have been more disposed toward despair, or at least indifference, regarding society's progress because they expected Christ's imminent return, rendering all human efforts superfluous. That movement of fundamentalists, now labeled the "New Christian Right,"[6] into the political forum has skewed the traditional differences between biblically conservative Christians with differing eschatologies. It is no longer possible to assume that premillennialism implies a "hands-off" attitude toward worldly affairs.[7]

Thus Southern Baptists may hold premillennial views of the eschaton and still work toward a more upright world here and now. Though they are unlikely to hold the postmillennial vision of ushering in the "kingdom of God," as a Christian reconstructionist might, they may use such views to bolster a social conservatism that seeks political and social stability in a world that must be evangelized. They are likely to emphasize individual rather than social conversion, but they still recognize the necessity of a stable—and to their minds traditional—social order.[8]

Likewise, one cannot assume any general acceptance of separatism. A premillennial eschatology and a general dissatisfaction with the secular "way of the world" suggest that fundamentalists want to separate themselves from the rest of society. In many instances this has been the case. Early fundamentalism was often apolitical, even antisocial. If the world could not be changed by human activity, Christians could at least keep themselves pure by avoiding unnecessary contact with it.[9]

6. See Bromley and Shupe, *The New Christian Politics*, and Liebman and Wuthnow, *The New Christian Right*.

7. Helen Turner claims that one major impetus for the success of the fundamentalist coalition in the SBC is an eschatology that characterizes America as "doomed" if it does not come back to Christ. Coalition leaders view the success of the fundamentalists both as correct interpretation of God's plan and as proper implementation of it. Of course, the force of that eschatological vision will recede as the coalition continues to retain power. See Helen Turner, "Myths: Stories of This World and the World to Come," in *Southern Baptists Observed*, ed. Nancy Ammerman (Knoxville: University of Tennessee Press, 1993).

8. Jeffrey Hadden, "Religious Broadcasting and the New Christian Right," *Journal for the Scientific Study of Religion* 26 (March 1987), 1–24.

9. Such a separatism is today more often practiced by those "literalists" found in Pentecostal sects. Though Pentecostals are almost always premillennialist, inerrantist, and separatist, it is interesting that we seldom think of them when we use the term "fundamentalist." There are likely two reasons for this. First, Pentecostals have always emphasized the changing nature of revelation and therefore have not exhibited the genuine conservatism associated with fundamentalism. Second, the public persona of Jerry Falwell and those like him in the New Christian Right have wrested the label "fundamentalist" away from any other form of biblical literalism. For an excellent discussion of American Pentecostalism, see Robert M. Anderson, *Vision of the Disinherited* (New York: Oxford University Press, 1979).

Fundamentalism can no longer be clearly identified by such separatism. With Christian schools for their children and a wide range of Christian social programs within the churches,[10] fundamentalists still manage to isolate themselves from the rest of the world to some degree.[11] Likewise, they seek to provide such stable "plausibility structures"[12] that their members are insulated from contamination when they do have contact with the secular world. But for most modern fundamentalists and even for sects or monastic orders, it is impossible in the late twentieth century to avoid nearly constant contact with a complex set of economic and political institutions. Those who try to do so are necessarily relegated to the margins of society. Most, however, including most of those we would classify as fundamentalist, are involved in an ongoing give-and-take between their own worldviews and those around them.[13] They may be more or less separate from other particular institutions or ideas, but they could hardly be called "separatist" in the sense historically reserved for such a definition.

Therefore, although Southern Baptist fundamentalists may seek to disassociate themselves and the denomination from certain alliances with groups they consider too secular[14] or profane, they do not seek to stop doing the "social" work these groups perform. Their concern is for internal control and direction more than for a cessation of contact altogether.

Finally, fundamentalists are evangelists. Their absolute allegiance to scrip-

10. It is not uncommon for large suburban churches to have their own "singles" programs, recreational activities, and even such specific ventures as Christian Weight Watchers or Christian pottery classes.

11. The best theoretical discussion of the practice of "isolation" and "insulation" in community-building is Rosabeth Moss Kanter's *Commitment and Community: Communes and Utopias in Sociological Perspective* (Cambridge, Mass.: Harvard University Press, 1982), esp. chap. 4.

12. I assume that Peter Berger's term now has such a wide currency in academic circles that little further exposition is necessary. I here mean simply that fundamentalists who participate in the wide range of programs offered by their churches have such consistency and continuity in their experience that their worldviews are able to withstand the stress of exposure to different or hostile views. See Peter Berger, *The Sacred Canopy* (Garden City, N.Y.: Doubleday, 1961; and Peter Berger and Thomas Luckmann, *The Social Construction of Reality* (Garden City, N.Y.: Doubleday, 1966).

13. James Hunter describes this process by using the term "cognitive bargaining," though he does not regard it as the "give-and-take" I do. See James Hunter, *American Evangelicalism* (New Brunswick, N.J.: Rutgers University Press, 1983). For Hunter, the bargaining is only between what fundamentalists will take from modernity and what they will not, with no account of what they may give in the intercourse. I shall return to Hunter and to the process he describes.

14. Even such groups as the Baptist World Alliance and the BJCPA, which most outside observers would consider decidedly unsecular.

ture requires them to be "saved" and to work for the salvation of others. Fundamentalists, to be sure, do not imagine that they "save" others themselves; their mission is to present the "gospel" to a lost world, fulfilling the "great commission."[15] The tension between such evangelism and the tradition of separatism—being in the world but not of it—produces an energy that manifests itself as both feverish activity and anxious hesitancy.[16]

The emphasis on evangelism may be even greater for many Southern Baptist fundamentalists because their own ecclesiological tradition is founded on mission work. To disassociate oneself from missions is, in the view of most Southern Baptists, to lose one's denominational identity. This tradition weighs so strongly in the life of the SBC that both separatist and premillennialist traditions are tempered by it.

Fundamentalists, both within and outside the SBC, can be identified as biblical conservatives who emphasize evangelism. They have premillennial eschatologies, yet many work for social change. They have low opinions of the secular world and often seek to insulate themselves from it, yet most have secular jobs and many live in pluralistic, cosmopolitan settings.

The Fundamentalist Paradox

Such ironies point up the "bargaining" position in which fundamentalists— and any sectarian group in modern, western societies—find themselves. They want to be "in the world but not of it," to change a world that is constantly changing them. Though I do not want to overstate (as is too often done) the inability of sectarian groups to make an impact on their environment, it is necessary to keep the impact the environment has on such groups clearly in mind. Bargaining works both ways. For instance, Moral Majoritarians *have* changed the debate about prayer in school, but their wishes are constantly revised and moderated by other perspectives, such that they may

15. The "great commission" (Matthew 28:19): "Go ye therefore and teach all nations, baptizing them in the name of the Father, and of the Son, and of the Holy Ghost."

16. Jerry Falwell has become the archetypal example of this "split" personality. On record as once disclaiming any political activity as a minister of the gospel, his name became synonymous with the New Christian Right and even with "fundamentalism." His recent actions imply something of a return to a position removed from secular political involvement. An excellent historical exposition of the many tensions in fundamentalism is George Marsden's "Preachers of Paradox: The Religious New Right in Historical Perspective," in Steven Tipton and Mary Douglas, *Religion and America* (Boston: Beacon Press, 1982).

achieve a "moment of silence" but will surely never arrange for a Christian prayer. Sectarian impulses did change the SBC, but they made these changes within a set of procedures—a polity—of which they were always and already a part.

Although there are serious tensions within fundamentalism, the movement as a whole places a much greater emphasis on the tradition of biblical authority than we expect to find in the modern world. It is natural, then, that such a reliance on scriptural guidance finds frequently itself at odds with bureaucratic structures that operate according to more rational, pragmatic rules, both within the SBC and within society as a whole. Likewise, a reliance on any singular, fixed authority must clash with a commitment to liberal, democratic ideas. And if the internal tensions mentioned earlier suggest that the movement has some of the same problems within that it seems to be fighting without, it does not necessarily mean that fundamentalism's insistence on biblical authority cannot still challenge the orders and authorities it considers secular.

The SBC is a forum where such a challenge has been successful. Inerrantists who believed that the denomination had become too liberal or too secular were able to push back against the advance of "modernization" precisely because they drew on traditions that were indigenous to the denomination.

Having said briefly *what* these fundamentalists believe, it is necessary to say a little about *who* they are and *where* they come from. Fundamentalists in the SBC today have a complicated heritage. They are both a recent, unique social movement responding to specific changes within their culture *and* descendants of a similar reactionary movement begun in the late nineteenth century. The distinction between "reactionary" and "conservative" is crucial here. Although the first American fundamentalists were biblically conservative, appealing to what they believed to be "traditional" views of scripture (that is, views that were precritical), their organization as a recognizable movement came in response or reaction to a perceived shift in their society's attitudes and mores.

If the world is always a changing place, a good argument can still be made that the late nineteenth-century world was changing at an unusually rapid pace. Central to these changes was a scientific worldview that took a hard and critical look at the assumptions of "natural law" prominent in the eighteenth-century writings of John Locke and Adam Smith. This new perspective challenged the notions of natural or traditional order, insisting on a closer examination of the role humans played in the world's grand scheme.[17]

17. Although this is an oft-rehearsed argument, I here follow the contours of an argument made by Ammerman in her "North American Protestant Fundamentalism," pp. 9ff.

Common acceptance of democracy signaled the end of the "divine right of kings." People not only demanded participation in their own governance but also began to assume it as their right. While it would be historically inaccurate to place the origins of democracy in the late nineteenth century (even the SBC's democratic roots were in seventeenth-century England), it is more plausible to find its widespread acceptance, or even assumption, here. Developments in the academy had done much to shift the "rights of man" from a bold assertion to an accomplished fact.

Though volumes have been written about such developments, two are especially worth noting. The first is the philosophical "turn to the subject," symbolized in the work of Immanuel Kant,[18] which moved the search for knowledge from the known to the knower. The idea of humans standing before a great world that they were to catalog, analyze, and seek to understand — in the traditions of Baconian science or a Lockean tabula rasa — was gradually replaced by an analysis of the way in which humans understood the world. Adam Smith's trust in an invisible hand and the deism of America's founders gave way to a philosophy that put the responsibility for the world's operation more squarely on the shoulder of human individuals.

The other important philosophical change began to move that responsibility beyond individuals to their societies. Sociologists advanced the idea that the key to understanding societies was in understanding the way humans worked together as groups. But this was *not* a matter of understanding the processes by which individuals acted and reacted to one another, or of discerning the work of Providence in their cooperation, but of understanding humans as social creatures whose individual actions are constituted by the group as much as they contribute to the group. The grandest statement of this view comes from Emile Durkheim, who insisted that "society" was a real entity in and of itself that comprised its individual units.[19]

Such contributions, although enormous in their impact, pale in the face of the work of Max Weber. It was Weber who in his seminal work *The Protestant Ethic and the Spirit of Capitalism* advanced the ideas that humans create social structures and that these structures appear to take on lives of their own, sometimes developing even against the will of their creators. It was Weber who first pointed up the processes of rationalization, noting that human interaction takes on certain predictable forms. In short, it was Weber

18. Immanuel Kant, *The Critique of Pure Reason; Critique of Practical Reason, and Other Ethical Treatises; The Critique of Judgement*, trans. John M. D. Meiklejohn (Chicago: Encyclopaedia Brittanica, 1990).

19. Emile Durkheim, *The Elementary Forms of the Religious Life*, trans. Joseph Swain (New York: Macmillan, 1915).

who had wrested control of the world not only from God, which arguably the work of subjective philosophy[20] and democratic ideology had already done, but also from the will of individual human agents.

Such work was being done in the "hard" sciences as well. Darwin has become symbolic of these changes for good reason. It is, in a very real way, Darwin's pioneering work into species survival that suggested an order that selected itself, rather than a carefully planned and executed blueprint of a Great Architect.[21] It was Darwin who came to represent the dominance of science over faith for many early twentieth-century Christians, a dominance that would endure.

Finally, these academic challenges to traditional order, the primacy of the individual, and even of God's omnipotence infiltrated the ranks of theology and biblical criticism. Perhaps nothing rankles fundamentalists more than the mention of "critical method" or "higher criticism," literary analyses used to discern both how and why the Bible is written as it is. Advances in historical and archeological work made it possible to separate pieces of biblical texts and to hypothesize about editorial combinations, additions, and subtractions. Long-accepted faith in ascribed authorship, either to Moses or to Christ's disciples, was rendered dubious. The traditional dating of "historical" incidents in the texts was challenged; in fact, the occurrence of several such events were relegated to the ranks of "mythology" or "folklore." While not necessarily contesting the divine inspiration of the canonical texts, modern biblical critics were able to say a great deal more about the human authors and the influence of their circumstances than had ever been said before.

When they did say it, they undermined the absolute authority of such texts for some observers. It is against this threat that fundamentalists reacted. In their view, either scriptural authority was sound or it was not. Gathering first in urban revivals (and not in the rural South), then in Bible and Prophecy conferences, and finally in organized denominational blocs, those who were disenchanted with the "advance" of culture stood against it, using the Bible as their support. They developed a unified resistance to the "modernizing" tendencies within their governments, their schools, and their

20. Kant surely never wanted to explain away God, but rather to understand him.

21. The Great Architect is an important deist concept used in the rituals of Freemasonry. While it is plausible for modern Christians, even conservative ones, to see evolution and natural selection as part of God's plan, there can be no question that such theories undercut not only the "literalist" reading of the Edenic myth but also any strict sense of God's complete control and manipulation of history.

churches. They formed transdenominational voluntary associations—such as Bible societies and mission organizations—and developed a wide body of literature, both books and periodicals. Gradually they developed their own educational institutions, including both independent seminaries and Bible colleges. The fundamentalists became a force for *change*, in this sense for a *return* to traditional[22] values, that had to be reckoned with.

In the 1920s it appeared that society had reckoned with them, with unfortunate consequences for the fundamentalists. The Scopes trial seemed to characterize fundamentalists as rural, backward southerners[23] trying desperately to cling to a past that no longer existed.[24] Fundamentalists were turned back in their challenges to the denominational establishment in the Presbyterian and Methodist churches, just as biblically conservative populism failed in the SBC.[25] Though their institutions and their literature still existed, as did their dissatisfaction, fundamentalists were pushed to the margins of American society as a whole.

It is from these margins that fundamentalists have reemerged more recently. After their "defeat" in the 1920s, fundamentalists seemed to turn to the "separatist" side of their identity, doing evangelical work within their own substantial base of institutions and literature. A complex combination of forces, both internal and external, have conspired to draw fundamentalists back into the "public" arena.[26]

22. Ammerman points out that these "traditional" norms were actually late nineteenth-century ones resembling little the "norms" of apostolic or medieval Christianity.

23. This characterization, although nearly lethal for fundamentalism as an intellectual movement, was unfair. The biblical conservatism of the South, and the reactionary fundamentalist movement in the Northeast, were not identical. There was considerably more cultural homogeneity in the South (Bryan did win at Dayton, to the delight of nearly all the locals); the derision came from the more cosmopolitan Northeast, perhaps best represented by Mencken's scathing coverage of the proceedings.

24. The literature on the Scopes "monkey trial" is extensive, but key to understanding the relationship of fundamentalism to what might be called "modernity." Books I have found helpful include L. Sprague De Camp, *The Great Monkey Trial* (Garden City, N.Y.: Doubleday, 1968); Norman Furniss, *The Fundamentalist Controversy, 1918–1931* (Hamden, Conn.: Archon Books, 1963); Willard Gatewood, *Controversy in the 1920s: Fundamentalism, Modernism, and Evolution* (Nashville, Tenn.: Vanderbilt University Press, 1969); Ray Ginger, *Six Days or Forever: Tennessee Versus John Thomas Scopes* (Boston: Beacon Press, 1958); John Scopes and James Presley, *Center of the Storm: The Memoirs of John T. Scopes* (New York: Holt, Rinehart & Winston, 1967); and Jerry Tompkins, *D-Days at Dayton: Reflections on the Scopes Trial* (Baton Rouge: Louisiana State University, 1965).

25. Furniss, *Fundamentalist Controversy*, is especially helpful on this point. To put this event in an even larger context, see Ahlstrohm's brief description of it in *A Religious History of the American People*, pp. 895ff.

26. Ammerman, "North American Protestant Fundamentalism," p. 40.

The social upheaval of the 1960s and early 1970s—especially the Vietnam war and the Nixon resignation—deeply strained Americans' faith in their basic institutions, especially the legislative and judicial branches. Equal rights for women, blacks, and homosexuals threatened what remained of the "traditional" structures fundamentalists (along with many other Americans) held dear. This erosion expanded to religious faith; people, especially young people, became religious "seekers" in large numbers. New constitutional limits on the prohibition of abortion and the eradication of prayer from schools pointed up, for many, the moral depth to which their society had been lowered.

If fundamentalists had failed to oppose these changes publicly, or been unable to get a hearing, it would surely have marked the end of their influence in American life. But they did speak out. Moreover, they gained not only a hearing but a larger following. Apparently it was not only a small band of biblical literalists who believed that society was overlooking their traditional values, but a substantial segment of the American population. Fundamentalists, represented most visibly by Jerry Falwell and his Moral Majority, began to push back at the "advances" of modern liberalism.

That they were able to do so signals not only their appraisal of the situation as desperate, but also their own internal strength. During their decades of silence since the 1920s, fundamentalists had experienced many of the same demographic changes as the rest of the nation—namely, they had become more urban and suburban and more wealthy. These factors did not, however, have the immediate consequence of "liberalizing" fundamentalists' view of the world, at least in the first generation. On the contrary, they strengthened their resolve in the face of the new cosmopolitan, pluralistic environment that confronted them. If anything, the ranks of fundamentalists grew during this migration because people who were simply biblically conservative became "fundamentalists," with the rigidity that term implies, as they moved from more homogeneous, rural settings into more heterogeneous, urban ones.[27] Fundamentalists had become more numerous and more wealthy. Their public strength grew accordingly.

Consequently, fundamentalists were able to make their case for traditional values not as ignorant hillbillies riding into town on wagons but as established members of the middle or lower-middle classes. They had education

27. Ammerman advanced, and later demonstrated through her study of the SBC, the thesis that the demographic groups most likely to have fundamentalist theologies consist of people who are rural by birth and background and those who have recently moved from rural to urban areas (of course, some fundamentalists leave urban areas for more rural ones).

(at least from their own institutions), they were literate, and they were well versed in the nature of society's problems. They offered their society an alternative to what they viewed as a foundationless heap of liberal ideas and aspirations.

What fundamentalists wanted was to bring America "back" to biblical, traditional values. However, the fact that they had entered the discussion at all suggests that there was, in fact, a discussion to be entered. American society was well past the point where fundamentalists could simply turn back the clock.[28] They had established, by their political clout, that they were a voice that deserved to be heard. What they had not established—indeed, what they could not establish—was that they were the *only* legitimate voice. If they wanted prayer in school, they were going to have to argue for it against the claims of civil libertarians, who also enjoyed public respect. If they wanted to teach creationism in schools either instead of or adjacent to the teaching of evolution, they were going to have to make a case for the merits of their position.[29] The rules of the game were set, and fundamentalists may have been able to participate in a way they could not before, but they could not change the rules.

What they were left with was an exercise similar to what Hunter has called "cognitive bargaining."[30] However, fundamentalists were not relegated to bargaining only for what they would "take" or "not take" from their environment. They offered ideas to the society, and some of those ideas met wide acceptance, changing the public perception of a particular problem.[31] At the same time, however, they were forced to modify their views to participate in the public arena. Most notably, as I have already claimed, they had to drop their demands for total or absolute compliance.

This is not to say that they necessarily had to abandon their core beliefs themselves. Hunter goes on to point out:

28. Frank Lechner, to whom I'll return, makes this point convincingly in his "Fundamentalism and Sociocultural Revitalization in America: A Sociological Interpretation," *Sociological Analysis* 46 (Fall 1985), 243–60, and his "Modernity and Its Discontents," in *Neofunctionalism*, ed. Jeffrey Alexander (Newbury Park, Calif.: Sage Publications, 1985).

29. Richard Stempien and Sarah Coleman, "Processes of Persuasion: The Case of Creation Science," *Review of Religious Research* 27 (December 1985), 169–77.

30. James Hunter, *American Evangelicalism* (New Brunswick, N.J.: Rutgers University Press, 1983), pp. 15–17, 134.

31. Perhaps the most "widely accepted" of these ideas is the notion that America is in a spiritual and moral crisis. Although fundamentalists have failed to line up the support they need to change social norms concerning abortion, homosexuality, or prayer in schools, they have paced the public concern over a loss of "values" in American life. While it is true that few have been able to agree on just what "values" we are failing to maintain, it is common to agree that some must be missing.

> Traditional beliefs, as long as they are firmly buttressed by a stable institutional matrix, can remain relatively protected from the world-disaffirming realities of modernity. There is, then, as much as one can tell, a future for orthodoxy in contemporary society. Yet for those concerned with doctrinal and religious purity, or with the expansion of the kingdom of God on earth, this future promises in the long term to be less than cheerful.[32]

Thus it is not that fundamentalists cannot continue to argue about particular values or legal decisions. They can continue the fight, as Donald Heinz puts it, for the symbols that fund our culture.[33] But what they cannot do is change the fact that they are fighting, or arguing, or "making a case" for their position in a forum that comprises a plurality of positions also assumed to be legitimate.

And while there can be little doubt that fundamentalists, again represented by the Moral Majority, struck a chord among a strand of discontented "traditionalists," it is no longer certain that their influence was as wide as once popularly believed. Recent studies suggest that the impact of the New Christian Right on the 1980 and 1984 elections was actually quite small; in the 1988 and 1992 elections the influence was smaller still.[34] Similarly, although the lasting impact of Ronald Reagan's policies and judicial appointments remains to be seen, the President was unable to return prayer to school, outlaw abortion, or institute many of the other policies his campaign rhetoric aimed at the New Christian Right promised. The candidacy of Pat Robertson, although it garnered significant press coverage, never posed a serious political challenge to the establishment either in Washington or in the Republican party.[35] In short, it is difficult to measure the cash value of many of the Moral Majority's cries for reform.

32. Hunter, *American Evangelicalism*, p. 134.

33. Donald Heinz, "The Struggle to Define America," in Liebman and Wuthnow, *New Christian Right*.

34. Erling Jorstad, *The New Christian Right, 1981–1988: Prospects for the Post-Reagan Decade* (Lewiston, N.Y.: Mellen Press, 1987), and Stephen Johnson et al., "Vote for a Christian Right Candidate" (Paper presented to the Society for the Scientific Study of Religion at Louisville, Kentucky, October 1987).

35. Jeffrey Hadden and Anson Shupe wrote frequently about Robertson's candidacy during this period (usually overstating his potential impact). See their paper "Is Pat Robertson About to Embarrass God?" (presented to the Society for the Scientific Study of Religion in Louisville, Kentucky, in 1987). See also Jeffrey Hadden and Anson Shupe, *Televangelism* (New York: Huff & Co., 1988).

Programs and Possibilities for the Fundamentalist Coalition

Biblical conservatives in the SBC, like their counterparts in other denominations, reawakened in the 1960s (the Elliott controversy having actually started in 1959). They had been allies of the "reactionary" movement in the North at the turn of the century and in the 1920s; indeed, they (along with other southern, rural inerrantists) bore the brunt of the public's ridicule after Bryan's humiliating victory at the Scopes trial. Frank Norris, the biblically conservative, populist Texan of the 1930s, was a Southern Baptist muckraker.

When the biblical conservatives within the Convention moved to center stage in the 1960s, however, they did not do so as representatives of a "solid" southern culture. They were not merely allied with their northern brothers and sisters in reaction against a "northern" problem. The liberals they wanted to challenge were within *their* own denomination; they were part of southern culture. Historical-critical method was destroying *their* institutions. The bureaucracy that threatened their freedom was *their* bureaucracy. The biblical conservatives within the SBC emerged in the 1960s as a reactionary movement against changes within their own specific culture. *They* were now fundamentalists, responding to a fallen society that was not just "out there" but "in here" as well.[36] The "society" that prompted their discontent had not fallen as far as society as a whole, but the problems they identified were the effects of modernization and liberalization nonetheless.[37]

Furthermore, it was not nearly so clear that fundamentalists would be here limited to "bargaining" with the worldviews they opposed. There was not an established set of "left" or "libertarian" positions in the denomination. And if liberty was an important Baptist distinctive, so too was the authority of scripture. There was no "constitution" as such, and no Supreme Court, to protect the rights of dissidents over against the traditionalist "majority."

36. Said Jerry Vines in a sermon on understanding truth literally: "I have a feeling that one of the reasons we're battling such worldliness in our Southern Baptist churches is that the truth of the imminent return of the Lord Jesus Christ is flickering very low in the hearts of Southern Baptist people" (Pastor's Conference, 1986 Annual Meeting, Atlanta, Georgia).
37. SBC fundamentalists were concerned with their denomination, but they were also part of the larger movement trying to change American society. However, their emergence as fundamentalists must be explained in terms of changes within their immediate culture. The relationship between this and their alliance with the older fundamentalist movement is interesting, but it must be understood as two different parts of the same puzzle.

Fundamentalists, it seemed, had a chance to do in the SBC what they could not do in American society as a whole: effectively return the group to biblical purity and traditional values while playing within "the rules."

The degree to which these fundamentalists wanted "purity" is subject to debate. Some, even here, seem only to have wanted to ensure that their voices would be heard among others.[38] Others wanted proportionate representation on boards and in seminaries, though there was widespread disagreement on what the proper proportions were. There can be no doubt, however, that a substantial segment of the new coalition did want purity; they had no intention of providing "equal access" to views that ran counter to what they considered the Convention's biblical presuppositions.[39] Perhaps the best example of this latter position is portrayed by the overtures of "peace" among the Convention's warring factions at the Dallas convention in 1985 and the establishment of the Peace Committee. Though the committee was, in accordance with the traditions of cooperation and democratic participation, established as "proportionate," there can be no doubt that it was weighted with a majority of fundamentalists. Therefore, its decisions were in many ways a foregone conclusion even though there was nominal discussion and debate on the issues. The resignation of moderate activists Cecil Sherman (*not* a biblical conservative in my sense) and Winfred Moore (very biblically conservative by almost any view), as well as the dissatisfaction of Chairman Charles Fuller all suggest that the "losing" side did not consider the process helpful.

This did not deter the coalition from using this process to bolster their commitment to purity. Jerry Vines, in a political statement before his election as president in 1988, said that he would appoint to committees only people who were "balanced within the parameters of the Baptist Faith and Message Statement . . . as interpreted by the Peace Committee, affirmed by

38. The purity versus parity debate raged long in the SBC. Fundamentalists claimed, correctly, that part of the problem was that their views were never represented by the old establishment. What is not clear, however, is whether those now in control want to institutionalize the "fairness" that was absent before or to acknowledge only the claims of those who are known to be biblically pure. The coalition has, to date, appointed only fundamentalists to fill vacancies.

39. James Draper advocates a "minimum irreducible theology" beyond which "diversity" will not be tolerated. It includes the deity and humanity of Christ; the substitutionary atonement; the literal bodily resurrection, ascension, and return; and justification through faith alone. These are, not surprisingly, very similar to "The Fundamentals" offered in the early twentieth-century origins of fundamentalism. *Baptist Press* release, April 27, 1988.

the convention sessions and interpreted by the Glorieta Statement of the seminary presidents."[40] While giving the appearance of being both cooperative and fair, in a democratic sense, Vines made it clear that he would appoint only inerrantists because only they, in his view, were "within the parameters of the Baptist Faith and Message Statement." The Peace Committee's work merely ratified the views of those already in power; they were able to interpret historical statements in light of their current agenda and to present them to the convention as "compromises" reached by a representative group of Baptist leaders.

Such activity may not have been perpetrated with the cynicism many moderates would like to ascribe; doubtless many of these fundamentalists genuinely believed they were carrying out the wishes of the denomination's majority. Pure motives or not, it is clear that the coalition's leadership intended to prosecute its program with extreme prejudice.[41]

Demographics of the Fundamentalist Coalition and Their Opponents

What is less clear is the degree to which the coalition's broad base of support—they had, after all, won every presidential election since 1979— shared this single-mindedness. As Ammerman's work has established, there are at least three, and possibly four, distinct "political" groups within the SBC from which the coalition claims support.[42]

The first of these are the "self-identified" fundamentalists, constituting 10 percent of the denomination. These people not only held biblical and theological positions that we might classify as fundamentalist, but also chose that term to describe themselves. It is very likely that those in this camp do support a program aimed at purity within the convention and that they are willing to manipulate the political process in the interest of that purity (i.e., are willing to stack the Peace Committee but still use it to claim "fairness").

The second group is the fundamentalist conservatives. This group, 22 percent of the denomination, shares theology and literalism with their counter-

40. *Baptist Press* release, May 12, 1988.
41. I mean this in the sense of single-mindedness of purpose, not implying any bigotry, racism, or hatred.
42. Ammerman, *Baptist Battles*, pp. 78ff.

parts above but chooses not to describe themselves as "Fundamentalist." While that distinction may seem trivial, additional data suggests otherwise. This group is, for instance, nearly half-again as likely (71 to 50 percent) as the self-identified fundamentalists to consider public education necessary to teach social cooperation. They are somewhat less likely than their self-identified fundamentalist brothers and sisters to be discontented with the denomination's bureaucracy, to want to punish churches that ordain women, or to leave the SBC should it get "too liberal" (though considerably more likely than the rest of the denomination to do any of these things).[43] It is clear that this group has supported the coalition's "correction" in the SBC, and probable that they will continue to do so. Lacking the self-understanding as "fundamentalist," however, they are not as single-minded in their pursuit of purity.

The third group from which the coalition draws support is the "conservatives," a whopping 47 percent of the denomination. These people, as most Southern Baptists (as is obvious given this range of numbers), are conservative in their biblical beliefs. But they are much more likely than self-identified fundamentalists to be content with the Convention's boards (25 to 8 percent) and very much less likely to leave should the Convention not make the corrections they deem necessary (22 to 55 percent). Although the coalition certainly does not draw support from everyone in this statistical bloc, even its supporters within this group do not share its level of discontent or its insistence on purity. And although nearly equal numbers of conservatives and fundamentalists share the view that SBC employees should believe and teach what most Baptists believe, reinforcing the idea that both groups have some interest in purity in their institutions, only 42 percent of conservatives would support measures to discipline those agencies for noncompliance (in this case for supporting women's ordination), while 77 percent of self-identified fundamentalists would. Thus a substantial agreement on theological and biblical principles does not necessarily imply an agreement on policy.

The "moderate-conservatives"—those who reject fundamentalist beliefs but still call themselves conservative (10 percent)—and the self-identified moderates (11 percent) clearly reject the policies of the coalition. But even they are biblical conservatives. Only 11 percent (perhaps not coincidentally the number of self-identified moderates) disagreed or strongly disagreed with

43. Ibid., chap. 4.

the statement "The scriptures are the inerrant Word of God, accurate in every detail." The accuracy and authority of scripture enjoy great allegiance from the bulk of Southern Baptists, even if the extent to which that produces support for policy change is uncertain.

Given that, anyone who wants to describe the SBC in terms of its tradition of democracy and cooperation, including the manner in which these led to the development of a large bureaucracy, must understand that the tradition of scriptural authority is a real, living, potent force. Though it may be intertwined now with both a complex system of democratic governance and a large-scale bureaucracy, it cannot be easily explained away or subsumed under either. Southern Baptists may be committed to democracy and to their institutions, but few Baptists would consciously say that either of these was ultimately more important than God's word.

In fact, most Southern Baptists are likely to believe that the authority of scripture will *solve* the democratic and bureaucratic problems the Convention is currently facing. James Draper's book on the subject, distributed to all the denomination's pastors, claims as much.[44] In Draper's view, the problem is not with the institutional structures themselves but in the unwillingness of the people who live within them to submit to the authority of the Bible. Having turned to the false authorities of denominational loyalty, modern scholarship, or their own power, denominational leaders have left the one tradition that can set them on the right course. The fact that Herschel Hobbs, the Southern Baptist patriarch and past-president who authored the Baptist Faith and Message, endorsed Draper's view (right on the book jacket) makes this view all the more plausible as a genuine strategy for renewal rather than a political tactic.

But whether "scriptural authority" is cited with goodwill or with intent to coerce, it carries a prestige in the denomination that seems, at least in Southern Baptists' self-appraisals, to outweigh any other claims to power. It is ostensibly, to the Southern Baptist mind, both the catalyst for and the locomotion behind the changes in the SBC since the early 1960s, and it will be the glue that holds the denomination together into the twenty-first century. It has coexisted with—some would say served as the foundation for—

44. James Draper, *Authority: The Critical Issue for Southern Baptists* (Old Tappan, N.J.: Fleming Revell, 1984): "I would suggest that the SBC, at one of its annual meetings, delegate to someone the authority to appoint a blue ribbon committee which would draw up such a set of parameters, and then present it for convention debate and possible adoption" (p. 108); "We cannot allow the cry of 'diversity' to intimidate us" (p. 109).

democratic and bureaucratic authority in the convention for nearly 150 years.

However, the changes in the South that helped to create the democratic and bureaucratic structures in the Convention, as well as the fundamentalist reaction to it, are not immediately responsible to scriptural authority. To say that the authority of the Bible is a real tradition that must be seen over against these others, even to say that Baptists identify it as the primary influence in their decision-making,[45] is not to measure either the extent or the effect of this influence. It is possible, even likely, that the loss of cultural homogeneity in the Convention foreshadows a corresponding loss of substantive agreement on what scripture "means." Thus, while the fact that so many Baptists claim that the Bible is authoritative is important, the degree to which this actually constitutes "agreement" is unclear.

The Bible has been a source of unity as well as controversy. In many ways it seemed, at least to Southern Baptists, to stand in judgment over other modes of authority. It represents at once both the sectarian impulse toward "priesthood of the believer," championing the notion of individual competence to interpret scripture, and the more doctrinal notion that if scripture's meaning is plain then some guidelines it sets for action must be obvious.

It is particularly interesting to note the ways in which the Bible has been used as an ally, and even a tool, at different points in the denomination's evolution. Reliance on scripture alone ("sola scriptura") was one of the first reasons that Baptists eschewed "churchly" denominations. It was just such an attitude, not so far removed from Landmarkism, that undergirded the fundamentalists' attack on bureaucracy and centralization in the SBC. It is also, however, the justification the fundamentalists use for promulgating more doctrinal pronouncements, for setting harder parameters for Southern Baptist life. It is not surprising that in the hands of moderates it is again the guardian of independence that challenges those pronouncements.

The Bible is the standard of truth and conduct for all Southern Baptists. But the power and authority of scripture in the Convention cannot be understood outside of the other contexts in which it is invoked.

---

45. I challenge this claim to biblical primacy in my paper "The Relationship of Belief to Institutional Location in Moral Decision-Making: The Case of the SBC" (Paper presented to the Association for the Sociology of Religion, Atlanta, Georgia, August 1988), to which I shall return.

5

Pastoral Authority and the Priesthood of the Believer

Two Traditions of Local Authority

Virtually all Southern Baptists, it would seem, are steeped in the Convention's tradition of democratic cooperation, even if they disagree about the organizational forms such cooperation should take. Further, Baptists are nearly unanimous in their endorsement of the tradition of biblical authority; most would go so far as to call the scriptures infallible and inerrant. These two traditions sometimes come into conflict. That conflict is exacerbated by the tradition of local church autonomy as it reveals itself simultaneously in the concept of "the priesthood of the believer" and in the person of the powerful, charismatic pastor.[1]

It is "exacerbated" because Southern Baptists seem most different at the local level. Although they share a widespread, general agreement about the authority of scripture and about democratic processes for group governance, those principles often look wildly different as they are played out in each

1. Many Southern Baptists will insist that the correct term is "priesthood of all believers." However, I have chosen "priesthood of the believer" because that was the phrasing of the resolution passed at the San Antonio meeting. Besides, the difference between these collective and individualistic notions is part of what is at stake.

local congregation. Some Southern Baptist churches are truly governed from the ground up; all decision-making is done by the membership, and the pastor is regarded as an employee, or servant, of the group. In other churches the pastor is a figure of absolute authority; the church's programs, and often even its buildings, are identified with him: it is "his" church.

There are, of course, many different kinds of churches that fall somewhere between the ideal-types of full congregational participation and absolute pastoral control. Understanding the current controversy in the Convention requires some familiarity with the sources of these different types of authority and their relationship to the other sources—scripture and democratic governance—already mentioned.

James Sullivan, author of the foundational *Southern Baptist Polity as I See It*, published a sequel of sorts in 1987: *Southern Baptist Polity at Work in a Church.*[2] His chapter titles tell his story: "A Spiritual Nature," "A Missionary Purpose," "A Biblical Base," "Led by the Pastor," "Supported by the Deacons," "Governed by the Congregation." As in his earlier work, Sullivan is almost Pollyannaish about the degree to which practice resembles theory. By 1987 it was ludicrous to assert, as Sullivan does, that

> congregational governance . . . is and always has been our way of life. We have never known anything else. To us it is made necessary by the nature of the church, the worth of persons and the Scripture passages which either allude to it directly or provide for the authority being placed in the hands of the congregation. This is different from those churches who put such powers in the pastor only or in another group of designated leaders who will make all the decisions for the church body.[3]

While this may have been the theory, the fact was that many Southern Baptist churches had vested a great deal of authority in their pastors. The fundamentalist leaders who had assumed positions of power in the denomination were known as men who exercised great control over the operation of their "super churches," and they did so with no apologies.

Indeed, they often criticized more moderate pastors for failing to win enough souls or to lead with enough conviction on matters of scriptural truth. Such a failure to provide spiritual guidance was, in the view of many

2. James Sullivan, *Southern Baptist Polity at Work in a Church* (Nashville, Tenn.: Broadman Press, 1987).
3. Ibid., p. 93.

fundamentalists, the root of the denomination's liberal problem.[4] Because of the Convention's congregational polity, no doctrinal control could be exercised over "weak" or unsound churches.

For their part, moderate pastors considered the fundamentalist leaders' tactics heavy-handed and unscriptural at best; at worst they called them demagoguery. They believed that scripture called for a governance coming more from the ground up (although the degree to which their churches mirrored this theory in practice surely differed) and that the "priesthood of the believer" was a hallmark of Baptist belief. To them such a priesthood meant that no believer stood above or below any other, or, more to the point, that none stood between any other and God.[5]

This doctrine meshed well with the moderate's liberal-democratic convictions. Better educated and better off, the moderates were most likely to claim individual autonomy—both for themselves and for their churches—as a "right." They often regarded their churches, like their other social organizations, as voluntary associations where like-minded people came together, in this case to worship.[6]

Because of their status, such people were accustomed to full participation in the decision-making processes that concerned them. Accordingly, they participated in their churches. Although the pastor was usually regarded as the "leader" in these churches, he was often regarded as an "employee" as well. He "led" in spiritual matters and was responsible for much of the program planning, but business decisions were made in business meetings open to all members (usually held in lieu of Wednesday-night prayer meetings once a month).[7]

Moderates regarded their rights to freedom of conscience and freedom of

4. Jerry Vines said in 1986 that when other Baptists got right with God they'd be where he was.

5. Baptist historian Bill Leonard, certainly a moderate, speaks of the "clergification" of the SBC. Of the authoritarian pastor Leonard says, "This model of ministry has typically characterized independent Baptist churches, but the model is becoming more normative in the SBC. It's more publicly visible in the so-called super churches, but it's also quite prevalent in smaller churches that see it as a way to grow into super churches. It makes the laity second-class citizens. It undermines the most basic biblical understanding of the church as the whole people of God" (*Baptist Press* release, June 3, 1988).

6. There is a strong element of individualism, akin to Troeltsch's mysticism, in most American religious life. See Robert Bellah et al., *Habits of the Heart: Individualism and Commitment in American Life* (Berkeley and Los Angeles: University of California Press, 1985).

7. Nearly all Southern Baptist churches hold such business meetings, but the degree to which initiative actually comes from the congregation and decisions are made at the grassroots level varies widely.

the local church from denominational control as articles of faith. These, to many moderates, were the key tenets of Baptist belief. Each had a *personal* relationship with Christ; each interpreted the plain truths of scripture for himself or herself. Each gathered with others who had similar relationships into a local body and participated in the corporate governance. This process usually involved seeking consensus or common consent, but democratic rules were invoked when agreement was not forthcoming. These churches then went on to cooperate with other churches in a similar fashion.

Fundamentalists did not directly challenge these "rights" of individuals or their churches, but neither did they wholeheartedly endorse them. They did not openly deny the rights of moderates to exercise democracy in the churches, but neither were they known for tolerating dissent in their own churches.[8] Placing too great an emphasis on each individual's interpretation of scripture seemed to many fundamentalists to invite misunderstanding and misapplication of biblical truth. It was one thing to say that each could read scripture for himself or herself; it was quite another to say that they might reasonably reach different conclusions about key points.

Some disagreement about interpretation was inevitable, and some toleration was therefore necessary.[9] But fundamentalists feared that moderates regarded the rights to "priesthood of the believer" and "local church autonomy" as license to believe and behave however they wanted—perhaps to interpret scripture metaphorically, to ordain women, to emphasize social programs over individual soul-winning—with doctrinal and denominational impunity. If any moderates did indeed think that way, they were half right.

Nothing fundamentalists could do or say would have doctrinal consequences for those they considered to be in error. There simply are no mechanisms for enforcing doctrinal control within the SBC polity. However, once fundamentalists were in charge of the denomination's institutional machinery the denominational costs of such error could be very high. If they could not force individuals or churches to think or act correctly, they could exclude those who thought wrongly from participating in the denomination's leadership. The "right" to one's own opinion was only a negative right; mod-

---

8. Charles Stanley publicly rebuked a woman who had questioned his decision to move the First Baptist Church of Atlanta to the suburbs, calling her "demon possessed." Homer Lindsey (Vines's co-pastor) said of the voting patterns of his church's messengers: "I am not going to tell you how to vote, but I know God has told me how to vote and He is not going to tell me one thing and you another."

9. Fred Wolfe, a fundamentalist leader, told me that he and Jerry Vines differed on many points of interpretation even though they were close personally. The important thing, he said, is that they did not differ on the key truths of scripture on which salvation hinged.

erates had the right to be free from doctrinal coercion, but this did not give them the right *to* anything.

It is interesting, almost ironic, to note that moderates were hoisted on their own petard. Committed as they were to the rights of individuals to believe as they wished, they could admit only that fundamentalists had a right to be biblical inerrantists. Committed as they were to democratic control, they could admit only that fundamentalists had a right to vote, and to win, at annual meetings. In fact, fundamentalists often pointed to the Convention votes as justification for their actions. As with the Peace Committee or the early votes on inerrancy, fundamentalists could legitimate their actions to moderates by pointing out that they had majority support.

Moderates were left with no option but to fight back, following the same rules, or to retreat. Confident that they were right about individual autonomy, and that most Baptists agreed with them, they used that issue to challenge the fundamentalists' position of greater pastoral control and the need for limits on individual interpretations of scripture.

Implications for the Polity: A Glimmer of Liberal Democracy

I mention the two together—pastoral control and limits on individual interpretation—because they fit hand-in-glove. The extreme moderate version of "priesthood of the believer"—that individual conscience is *the* ultimate authority in scriptural interpretation—requires a polity that is participatory, even democratic. In a parallel fashion, fundamentalists' insistence on the need for theological parameters, or limits, suggests an authority that is capable of discerning and maintaining those limits. The question is not whether there is general agreement about what the Bible says; the question is, finally, about who decides. The denomination's left and right wings disagree vigorously on the answer to that question.

This disagreement is crucial because nothing separated the two emerging parties in the Convention more than this difference on pastoral versus individual authority. This debate came to a head, with telling consequences, at the 1988 annual meeting in San Antonio. The moderate candidate for president was Richard Jackson, a known inerrantist. That moderates had chosen Jackson now for the second year, as they had chosen Winfred Moore in the two preceding years, signaled their recognition of the Convention's biblical conservatism. If they could not hope to win support for more progressive views on biblical interpretation and social issues, they might at least be able to assert their rights to hold those views while still participating as loyal Southern Baptists. If the most "moderate," or liberal, members of the denomination could not claim leadership roles in the Convention, they might at least be able to remove the fundamentalists so that more tolerant conservatives, like Jackson, could lead.

Jackson's pre-Convention rhetoric reveals this strategy. Striking not at "theological parameters" but at pastoral control, he called the fundamentalist coalition's leaders "high priests." The *Baptist Press* offered this report of a Jackson speech: "Southern Baptists are abandoning one of their cherished doctrines—the priesthood of the believer—by surrendering control of their denomination to a handful of 'high priests.' "[10] Jackson went on to make the point even more clearly:

> The conflict, he says, is a struggle for priesthood—whether individual, free-thinking Southern Baptists will determine the direction and nature of their denomination or whether those powers will reside in a handful of leaders.[11]

With such charges, moderates hoped to bring back a spirit of toleration to the Convention's leadership, even if that toleration now admitted a much more widespread acceptance of inerrancy than it had before.

Jerry Vines, the candidate of the fundamentalist coalition, was equally blunt. The denomination's "correction" toward some theological limits needed to continue, and that required, in his view, "a courageous conservative."[12] The new president needed to use his appointive powers to make certain that no one enters denominational leadership who does not subscribe to the inerrant interpretation of the Baptist Faith and Message as delivered by the Peace Committee.

The two men could not have drawn the lines more clearly. That the Convention was biblically conservative was now certain, as both men agreed. But one wanted that conservatism to express itself through the beliefs of each individual, and the other wanted a strong leader, a "courageous conservative," to enforce such ideas in the hierarchy. The messengers, it seemed, had a clear choice.

10. *Baptist Press* release, May 12, 1988, paraphrasing Jackson.
11. Ibid.
12. Ibid.

Their vote did not, however, offer any equally clear resolution. Vines won, but by the narrowest margin imaginable. Out of 31,291 votes cast, the margin of victory was 692 votes (another 358 messengers voted for two alternative candidates).[13] The fundamentalist agenda would remain intact, but this vote suggested a potential crack in their armor.

The fundamentalists were not magnanimous in their victory. Although they could not be sure whether the closeness of the vote signaled dissatisfaction with their tactics, genuine disagreement about the role of individual and pastoral authority, or simply respect for Richard Jackson (whose church often leads the denomination in Cooperative Program giving and baptisms), they wanted to bolster their position while still maintaining an apparent majority. If they could not eliminate the doctrine of "priesthood of the believer," they could downgrade it. By doing so they could kill three birds with one stone: (1) they would have the Convention's approval for their continued program; (2) they would defuse any future attacks, like Jackson's, based on assertions about their opposition to that doctrine; (3) they could establish that Jackson's support had been personal, not issue-oriented.

The fundamentalists had no ecclesiastical authority to establish or repudiate any doctrine. The opposition could continue to believe and to promote any views they wanted to. Fundamentalists could, however, do what is for Southern Baptists the next best thing—they could pass a resolution. While this would not have any binding authority over individuals in their local churches, it would establish conclusively that the Convention supported the types of changes under way despite what Richard Jackson and the moderates might say.

This resolution, championed on the convention floor by coalition leader Fred Wolfe, was passed on the Wednesday after Vines's election:

RESOLUTION NO. 5
ON THE PRIESTHOOD OF THE BELIEVER

Whereas, None of the five major writing systematic theologians in Southern Baptist history have given more than passing reference to the doctrine of the priesthood of the believer in their systematic theologies; and

Whereas, The Baptist Faith and Message preamble refers to the priesthood of the believer, but provides no definition or content to the term; and

13. *SBC Annual, 1988*, p. 61.

Whereas, The high profile emphasis on the doctrine of the priesthood of the believer in Southern Baptist life is a recent historical development; and

Whereas, The priesthood of the believer is a term which is subject to both misunderstanding and abuse; and

Whereas, The doctrine of priesthood of the believer has been used to justify wrongly the attitude that a Christian may believe whatever he so chooses and still be considered a loyal Southern Baptist; and

Whereas, The doctrine of the priesthood of the believer can be used to justify the undermining of pastoral authority in the local church.

Be it therefore RESOLVED, That the Southern Baptist Convention, meeting in San Antonio, TX, June 14–16, 1988, affirm its belief in the biblical doctrine of the priesthood of the believer (1 Peter 2:9 and Revelation 1:6); and

Be it further RESOLVED, That we affirm that this doctrine in no way gives license to misinterpret, explain away, demythologize, or extrapolate out elements of the supernatural from the Bible; and

Be it further RESOLVED, That the doctrine of the priesthood of the believer in no way contradicts the biblical understanding of the role, responsibility, and authority of the pastor which is seen in the command to the local church in Hebrews 13:17, "Obey your leaders, and submit to them; for they keep watch over your souls, as those who give an account;" and

Be it finally RESOLVED, That we affirm the truth that elders, or pastors, are called of God to lead the local church (Acts 20:28).[14]

Not only had Vines defeated Jackson, the most successful pastor the moderates could offer, but the fundamentalist preference for pastoral authority was elevated above individualistic notions of "priesthood." The moderates were shaken. In a fit of rebellious anger, some of them marched to the Alamo singing "We Shall Overcome."

The images such a "freedom march" evokes are appropriate. The most "progressive" elements in the denomination now had no choice but to view themselves as a minority concerned about protecting their right to participate in the larger polity. They were forced to admit the possibility that most

14. Ibid., pp. 68–69.

Southern Baptists did not give the same priority to "individualism" that they did.

For that reason the Alamo may have been an inappropriate destination. The small band of "freedom fighters" there lost the battle (indeed, they were annihilated), but their side won the war. After San Antonio, moderates had even less reason to be optimistic about their long-term chances. Those for whom spiritual individualism, the priesthood of the believer, had been a cornerstone of Baptist identity now had to reassess their future in the denomination. Losing the debate over the nature of authority at this most personal level had struck a blow from which some moderates might never recover. Admitting that the SBC did not value the individual's spiritual autonomy above all else was more than the most liberal Southern Baptists could stand. Losing votes and admitting the denomination's biblical conservatism was one thing; officially endorsing a limitation on SBC tolerance was another.

The 1988 annual meeting could be interpreted by moderates in two ways. On the one hand, they came closer to winning the presidency than they ever had. On the other, liberal ideas of pastoral and individual authority were seriously challenged. Moderates were forced to choose which of these trends seemed the more important; their future was now a matter of interpretation.

That choice was informed by other denominational facts about which such interpretation was no longer necessary. First, moderates had to admit that "spiritual individualism" was not as highly valued in the SBC as they thought. This is not to say that messengers to the Convention did not still consider themselves independent; they surely did.[15] But they were independent people who generally believed that some truths of scripture were beyond individual challenges. Independence is important, but biblical correctness is too.[16]

This suggests the second, corollary fact: the SBC values uniformity on certain biblical truths much more than some moderates had previously believed. The chickens of the early 1960s were coming home to roost in the 1980s; fundamentalists had gone beyond resolutions endorsing inerrancy, which they could not enforce for individuals, to resolutions supporting strong pastoral authority in the interpretation of scripture. They had not

15. My favorite moment at the 1989 meeting in Las Vegas came when a messenger moved that, for propriety's sake, resolutions and motions not be greeted with applause. His motion was roundly applauded.

16. Although there is no data that could help to measure such a claim, the fact that most messengers are pastors probably weighs their decisions in the direction of pastoral authority in interpreting scripture.

only filled the denomination's bureaucracy with those who shared their scriptural views, they had also, by passing this resolution, established that such actions had the denomination's consent.

Finally, moderates had by default conceded the SBC's preference for strong, charismatic pastors. Richard Jackson's church in Phoenix is one of the largest in the SBC, baptizing hundreds and giving more than $1 million to the Cooperative Program annually. Winfred Moore, the first real candidate of a publicly organized moderate effort, was less charismatic but still an influential conservative from a large, wealthy Texas church. Daniel Vestal, the candidate in 1989 and 1990,[17] emerged as a bright, young pastor who advocated more tolerance than the fundamentalists while still sharing their biblical conservatism.

In short, the moderates recognized that they needed to "run" men who could match the fundamentalists' candidates in preaching, church growth (and size), and personal charisma. The difference, the moderates insisted, is that their men were more tolerant of opposing views, less subservient to a "party" line, and more involved in the denomination's cooperative efforts.[18]

Implications for the Future of SBC Polity

At least through 1989, those distinctions were not persuasive. One possible reason is the difficulty in maintaining that one is both more cooperative and more independent. Many Baptists may have feared the idea of a core group within the fundamentalist coalition[19]—Jackson's high priests—but their votes indicated that they feared or resented the "good old boy" mentality of the former establishment even more. There had always been a "party line" of some sort, and most messengers felt more comfortable with the new one for the present.

Another reason might be that it is difficult to prove that men who are

17. In an unprecedented move, Vestal announced his 1990 candidacy in 1989, naming a slate of running mates as well.

18. At the Las Vegas meeting in 1989, the Vestal camp produced some straightforward campaign literature comparing the Cooperative Program giving (percentages and amounts) of the churches led by Vines, Rogers, Stanley, Jackson, and Vestal. Although the intent was to put the fundamentalists in a negative light, I heard at least as many negative comments about the open campaigning as I did about the fundamentalists' giving.

19. Every year, questionnaires came back to the Center for Religious Research pointing out Pressler and Patterson as the "bad guys" responsible for the controversy in the Convention.

pastors of churches with thousands of members and multimillion-dollar budgets are being manipulated by some doctrinal conspiracy. The Convention presidents since 1979 have surely been like-minded, but there is every reason to believe that they were equally so before 1979. It seemed unfair to many to accuse them of a conspiracy because they had decided to organize.

Accusations about fundamentalists' weak cooperation in the Cooperative Program did not carry the weight moderates expected. Given their concerns about the bureaucracy and the seminaries before the mid-1980s, it seemed natural that fundamentalists would give more to their own programs or to independent schools. Although this may have made fundamentalists seem less loyal to the denomination, moderate leaders never seemed to realize that, in this era of suspicion of the establishment, such loyalty was as much a liability as an asset.

Given all those facts, moderates were forced to decide their future. Those for whom absolute individual freedom of conscience and full participation in the organization were of supreme importance could find little satisfaction.[20] These have begun to pursue other avenues of cooperation and participation, first through the fledgling Southern Baptist Alliance and now through the Cooperative Baptist Fellowship (CBF). Ammerman, now a leader in the CBF, has called the Alliance meetings the "birth pangs of a new kind of Baptist,"[21] and the description seems apt: it is unlikely that in the foreseeable future the SBC will provide the opportunities for leadership and participation such people will require. This group, perhaps 5 to 10 percent of the SBC, will probably move gradually away from involvement in the denomination's programs. If they do not disaffiliate entirely, they will at least find other avenues for the bulk of their gifts and participation. But it would be unfair to write off all nonfundamentalists, or even most of them, based on such predictions. Much of the opposition to the fundamentalist coalition has come from biblical conservatives who share the fundamentalists' concerns about liberalism. Most, like Richard Jackson, shared the fundamentalists' frustrations about the old establishment and welcomed the denomination's conservative turn. Their opposition was primarily based on fears that the

20. The earliest moderates, such as Cecil Sherman, have long found themselves outside the boundaries of denominational discussion. When the "Gatlinburg Gang" first organized as opposition to the fundamentalists, they doubtless imagined that the battle hinged on the priority of individual freedom or biblical uniformity. The ensuing ten years have established conclusively that the Convention interprets freedom and tolerance in terms of scriptural truth and not vice versa. Those most committed to "freedom" found themselves pushed aside first by the fundamentalists and then by the more pragmatic, centrist moderates.

21. Ammerman, *Baptist Battles*, p. 285.

fundamentalists had been too exclusive and too heavy-handed; they preferred a program that was broader and more conciliatory.

These centrists[22] are unlikely to leave. They may or may not have associated with Southern Baptists Committed in the early going. They may have remained independent conservatives, perhaps watching quietly, perhaps opting to stay and fight. They accepted the denominational "facts"—less emphasis on individual autonomy, more biblical uniformity, strong pastoral authority—that seemed to be pushing their moderate siblings out of the denomination. Whether they have accepted, or can accommodate, any single-minded, exclusive strategy for the SBC remains to be seen. This group, the more conservative among the former Southern Baptists Committed members and those in the conservative middle concerned about the fundamentalists' exclusivity, will probably be the source of any future challenges to the coalition. As the struggle over pastoral versus individual authority in scriptural interpretation shows, the fundamentalists have "won." Correct—inerrantist—interpretations of key points of scripture have become the Convention's standard for measuring the performance of their institutions and their employees. Those for whom this standard is unsatisfactory have been forced to the edges of the denomination and may soon find themselves outside it. However, neither the move toward greater biblical uniformity nor a move away from absolute individual autonomy signals unqualified, or unending, success for the fundamentalist coalition. Their "corrections" in the denomination's course have been widely accepted. Some further initiatives to move the denomination to the theological or political right may also find acceptance, but there is reason to believe that not all such moves will receive unqualified approval.

One reason for saying this is the tenuous nature of the balance between pastoral and individual authority in interpretation of scriptures. Although the coalition turned back the more radical interpretations of "priesthood of the believer," they did not eliminate the doctrine entirely (nor did they try to do so). Southern Baptists, including fundamentalists, cherish the notion that salvation is a matter between an individual and God (through Christ). The "relationship" to Christ is described as "personal"; nothing could be more individualistic. Therefore, fundamentalists might successfully insist on certain key scriptural boundaries, but they run great risks when they try to form scriptural guidelines beyond those boundaries.

22. "Centrist" is a fuzzy term in the SBC. Some moderates preferred this term during the heat of the controversy. I use it now to describe biblical conservatives who are not particularly political, either in the denomination or in secular forums.

The Limits of Membership

Of course, the location of those "boundaries" is often difficult to discern. When asked to name which actual differences in interpretation should be tolerated, fundamentalists often mention differences in views on the eschaton.[23] However, on such matters as women's ordination or hiring divorcées as pastors or missionaries, they are less clear. Some say that these practices are up to the local church but that the denomination's institutions should toe the conservative line. Others, while not denying the right of local church to act as it chooses, refuse to associate with churches who engage in such practices.[24]

Clearly, Draper's "irreducible minimum" for theological soundness is not a fixed point. Moreover, one set of standards may apply to local churches and another to denominational institutions. The boundaries, it would seem, are subject to tinkering and debate. Although it is now clear that views of scripture that are not "conservative" are unwelcome in the Convention, the range of views that *will* be accepted is by no means clear.

That uncertainty makes the situation of the fundamentalist coalition precarious. They have succeeded in running the most far left wing of the denomination[25] out of positions of denominational power or influence, but if they have any aspirations beyond that they can expect greater resistance. Actual practice in most Southern Baptist churches falls somewhere between the poles of absolute pastoral authority and absolute individual autonomy.[26] The pattern for integrating the two will differ from church to church; the degree of compromise between them that will characterize the whole denomination is a matter of ongoing debate.

Fundamentalists used such a debate within the messenger process, insisting on their right to speak, to implement their programs in the Convention. Having done so, however, they are now subject to the same sorts of pressures

23. Draper, *Authority*, pp. 105–6, cites such differences as evidence of diversity. Several fundamentalist pastors we have interviewed also cite premillennialism/postmillennialism/amillennialism as "tolerable" differences.

24. The most notable example of this was the disfellowshiping of Prescott Memorial Baptist Church in Memphis, Tennessee, from the local association for calling Nancy Hastings Sehested as their pastor.

25. One should never lose sight of the fact that the "left" wing of the SBC merely holds to those views of higher criticism and metaphorical understandings that would be "centrist" in most Protestant groups.

26. I intentionally do not call this a dialectic relationship, because I mean to suggest a compromise rather than some new, third thing produced by this polarizing tension.

they applied. Although they succeeded in downgrading the notion of the "priesthood of the believer" such that individualism was shown to have limits, they did not—and could not—erase the strong tendency toward autonomy in the denomination. Southern Baptists were still independent; they were simply independent people who had asserted themselves as biblically conservative. They might have accepted a fundamentalist coalition to achieve a change of direction in the denomination, but they were not likely to be willingly manipulated or ordered about by it.

It is important to note, as some observers have failed to do, that the resolution concerning the "Priesthood of the Believer" was more about membership than about rights. It said that such a doctrine did not mean that anyone could "believe whatever he so chooses and still be considered a loyal Southern Baptist." In so doing it unofficially limited true, or full, membership in the denomination; those who invoked this doctrine "wrongly" ought not to expect to be fully participant.[27] Even the language concerning pastoral authority, in this context, seems aimed more at legitimating parameters or guidelines than at granting pastoral license. As the resolution kept the matter of pastoral authority squarely within the local church, it did not change the nature of the denomination's decision-making. If such a resolution undercut "democracy" or "grassroots participation" in the separate congregations, it did not do so in the Convention as a whole.

Therefore, those who are "members" of the Convention, those within the hazy biblical parameters of the group, can expect to exercise their rights in the body's decision-making. As members, they can insist on participation and inclusion in the denomination's programs; we should expect that the new leadership will, as politics demand, accommodate that insistence.

In an odd way, disagreement about local authority had a greater impact on the national organization than did disagreements focused at the national level. It was in these debates about individual versus pastoral authority that the denomination's answers to questions about democracy and interpretation

27. I am working here with Michael Walzer's notion that the community or group itself is a good to be distributed. He says that "membership cannot be handed out by some external agency" (including, I would add, some external principle) but that "its value depends on an internal decision." He continues: "Were there no communities capable of making such decisions there would in this case be no goods worth distributing" (Michael Walzer, *Spheres of Justice: A Defense of Pluralism and Equality* [New York: Basic Books, 1983], p. 29). I am claiming that the SBC made several decisions about what it meant to be a member of the group (although these only informally "enforced" membership privileges) and that those affected—fundamentalist, centrist conservative, conservative moderate, or liberal moderate—have reacted accordingly.

of scripture took shape. Members decided that key points of doctrine were the essence of what it was to be Southern Baptist; those who had considered that essence to be individual freedom of interpretation could only be dismayed.

But the fact that the debate ended as it did—the fundamentalists won and the most "moderate," or liberal, elements lost—does not necessarily mean carte blanche for fundamentalists in the future. If a small percentage of Southern Baptists now find themselves outside the new, informal standards for membership, we must remember that the great bulk of Southern Baptists still find themselves inside. Many, indeed most, of those members do not consciously align themselves with the fundamentalist coalition, although the large majority of messengers at annual meetings now seem comfortable with the new arrangements.

A new type of consensus, more scriptural than cultural, now undergirds the Convention's precarious democracy. That fundamentalists have succeeded in setting the new rules for the game is clear. That they have used those rules to win stunning victories is clear too. That the new rules, the new game, will benefit the SBC as it moves into the twenty-first century is much less certain.

6

The Bureaucracy and a
New Set of Rules

Membership in the New Polity

The new "consensus" in the Southern Baptist Convention might seem, at first glance, much like the old: it is based on certain shared presuppositions about the Bible, and it separates Southern Baptists from "others." It sets the boundaries for membership in the group, acting as a gatekeeper for "full" participation in the denomination.[1]

Despite these similarities, though, this new consensus cannot function as the old. At the turn of the century, Southern Baptists shared a much broader range of regional, cultural, and ideological experiences, which certainly included understandings of scripture but were never limited to them. Therefore, while scripture may have served as one means of designating membership, it was one means intimately intertwined with others. One was a Southern Baptist primarily because one was part of "Baptist" culture.[2]

1. I say "full" participation in order to distinguish it from "legal" participation. There are many within the Convention, especially the most liberal elements, who may still participate at annual meetings in accord with the rules of the denomination but who are not regarded, either by fundamentalists or by biblically conservative centrists, as candidates for positions of leadership or influence.

2. Although I believe that even in the 1970s Samuel Hill may have overstated the case for

Although it would be futile to argue that Southern Baptists do not, on the whole, still share certain demographic characteristics, there can be little question that such a base has been widely expanded. In matters of racial and cultural pluralism, Baptists in Arizona have experiences different from Baptists in Mississippi; rural Baptists have experiences different from urban Baptists. The South is no longer homogeneous, no longer "solid," and Southern Baptists could not be accurately identified only with southern culture even if it were.

Scriptural boundaries are therefore called on to do the work once done by a wide range of cultural and demographic factors. One is known to be a true Southern Baptist by one's assent to a few key doctrinal points. These may include belief in a great deal of individual freedom, but as we have seen, that freedom is itself always subject to other biblical limitations. It is not surprising that we can locate the Convention's current tensions at the places where these scriptural boundaries come under the greatest stress. The questions become "Who is a true Baptist?" and "What are the limits of exclusion (or inclusion)?" An abbreviated sort of "consensus" may help to determine membership, but the process is not an easy one.

Even if the boundaries of membership can be determined, there has been a significant, and irreversible, change in what it means to be a "member" of the SBC. If the past decade has indeed been a process of setting those boundaries and "weeding out" those who do not fall within them, that process has been termed both "war" and "politics."[3] Given the Convention's history of different sorts of democratic participation, the latter seems more appropriate. The process has always been democratic and therefore "political," but its politicization has taken a decidedly competitive turn, putting a new emphasis on the rights of members and individual choice. If the denomination can find ways to limit membership, can those who are members any longer think of themselves as other than individual players on a liberal, political stage?

To ask such a question is not to ask whether Southern Baptists, or even the messengers more specifically, will think of themselves primarily as voters

---

cultural solidarity in the South, his observation that "the white Southerner must belong to the church for the sake of establishing the legitimacy and solidarity of his culture" seems well placed. I would argue that the urban and rural distinctions had already begun but that in each religious membership—which in the South continues to mean Baptist membership first and foremost—stands as a bulwark against the encroachment of pluralism and cosmopolitanism. See Hill et al., *Religion and the Solid South*, p. 54.

3. Roy Honeycutt labeled the Convention's controversy a "holy war," a fact much noted by commentators of all sorts.

or candidates. Some will, but many will not. The question is whether Southern Baptists, especially the messengers, can avoid thinking of such political categories as a valid, necessary part of their denominational roles.[4] I contend that they cannot.

Even if diversity can be limited by the scriptural boundaries mentioned above, there have now been recognizable "parties" that fell within those boundaries. The governance of the Convention is now, as it has always been, handled by vote. The difference is the democracy that was once based on consensus or common consent can now be, as it recently has been, based on a model of competing interests. Consensus may still shape the "parameters" of membership, but it is no longer assumed to guide the denomination's actions.[5] The Convention's leaders are recognized as members of particular groups within the denomination, and though they speak "for" all Southern Baptists as the President of the United States speaks for all Americans, it is wrong to assume that their opinions always represent the thoughts or feelings of the whole. They may function as the voice of the Convention, but their views can only be known to represent a *majority*, not the entirety.

To be a Southern Baptist is now to be a part of the ongoing deliberation and debate about the Convention's programs and about its boundaries. To be a messenger at an annual meeting is to "take sides" whether one wishes to or not, whether one is ideologically consistent or not. The democratic process between contending parties with competing interests has been established as the mode of governance in the denomination as a whole. It is difficult to imagine that such a process could ever be reversed, returning true cultural or social consensus to the central role in decision-making.

Such a possibility would require that the "parameters" for membership be drawn so tightly that a new homogeneity could be achieved. While that is not technically impossible, it would require a gigantic system of revisions and reforms. Given that those reforms would themselves require democratic approval from the current, less homogeneous group, there is no compelling reason to expect them in the foreseeable future.

More compelling is the expectation that the Convention will continue as a forum for the many interests and ideas that can reasonably fall within the

4. For more on the idea of categories and institutional "roles," see Berger and Luckmann, *The Social Construction of Reality*, pp. 56ff., and Erving Goffman, *The Presentation of Self in Everyday Life* (1956; reprint, Garden City, N.Y.: Doubleday, 1959).

5. I use the term "parameter" because it is more often used by Draper and the other fundamentalist leaders. It is important to acknowledge that on this point they have won, even if their victory has been informal and nondoctrinal.

parameters of a rather loose doctrine of inerrancy. Although "loose inerrancy" may seem an oxymoron, it is not likely that any particular view of
inerrancy—beyond a few key doctrines—could be enforced in the Convention.[6] Those accepted as full members will continue to shape their denomination and its programs by their votes, both directly and through their enormous bureaucracy.

The 1991 annual meeting in Atlanta exhibited the sort of unity that seems
likely to emerge as the dust settles on the crisis. Morris Chapman, elected in
New Orleans in 1990, won a second term by unanimous approval. Few votes
were contested, and relatively little time was spent on political or parliamen-
tary matters.

Organizational Limits in the New Polity:
Bureaucratic and Democratic

In both democratic and bureaucratic processes, the limits on the fundamentalists' reforms became evident. Their success in setting the parameters for
membership could not be easily translated into programs that are as exclusive
or as pure as the most ideologically committed might like. Mechanisms
within those processes themselves, as well as diversity and independence
within the new biblical consensus, make the continuation of single-party
authority unlikely.

That the growth of the bureaucracy within the SBC paralleled the Convention's numerical and regional growth should come as no surprise. Weber
taught us that large, heterogeneous, democratic organizations cannot function adequately using the small-scale self-governance of local, homogeneous
democracies. A large democracy must develop regular mechanisms for performing its various functions. According to Max Weber, "This results from
the characteristic principle of bureaucracy: the abstract regularity of the ex-
ecution of authority, which is a result of the demand for 'equality before the
law' in the personal and functional sense . . . and the principled rejection of
doing business 'from case to case.'"[7]

As the SBC grew, it required large, predictable institutions to run its mas-

6. As I have said, just what those doctrines will include is still a matter of debate, although
they are sure to include biblical creation, the virgin birth, the bodily resurrection, and the
literal return of Christ.
7. Max Weber, "Bureaucracy," in *From Max Weber*, p. 224.

sive programs. As I suggested earlier, these institutions mirrored the social arrangements already familiar to those within the denomination, especially those who were most educated, urban, or wealthy.[8] The South's emerging middle class expected to participate in such bureaucratic and democratic organizations.

Peter Berger suggests yet another reason for such bureaucratic growth. He describes the ongoing spread of bureaucratic control in terms of what he calls "success-orientation."[9] Local congregations, regardless of polity, expect their central organizations to perform well the tasks they have assigned them.[10] For political and economic reasons, "(e)ach board, commission or committee seeks to perpetuate itself, to enlarge its importance within the total organization, and to justify its budget. These goals require 'success' in the activities allocated to the agency in question within the organization."[11]

It is important to remember, as some occasionally forget, that these bureaucracies do not merely *appear* to be successful. They are, in fact, successful in performing their assigned tasks and in garnering support for their programs both with a carrot (continued success) and a stick (exerting pressure on local congregations through whatever formal or informal means exist).[12]

For all the talk of Weber's pessimism about rationalization and bureaucracies, we must remember that he considered their efficiency and precision to be very real. He first described the "cage" of bureaucracy and technology as iron precisely because it is so hard and immoveable.[13] "The decisive reason for the advance of bureaucratic organization has always been its purely technical superiority over any other form of organization. The fully developed

8. John Meyer and Brian Rowan have argued that organizations are "driven to incorporate the practices and procedures defined by prevailing rationalized concepts of organizational work and institutionalized in society. Organizations that do so increase their legitimacy and their survival prospects, independent of the immediate efficacy of the acquired practices and procedures" ("Institutionalized Organizations: Formal Structure as Myth and Ceremony," *American Journal of Sociology* 83 [March 1977]).

9. Peter Berger, *The Noise of Solemn Assemblies* (Garden City, N.Y.: Doubleday, 1961), pp. 163ff.

10. The earliest SBC was nothing more than a group of "societies," each with a specific task.

11. Berger, *Noise of Solemn Assemblies*, p. 164.

12. Berger mentions personal persuasion and the withholding or granting of funds. One must remember Harrison's point that the executives in an "informal" power structure, like the SBC's, often wield *more* power than an ecclesiastical authority, precisely because they have no formal constraints.

13. See Max Weber, *The Protestant Ethic and the Spirit of Capitalism*, trans. Talcott Parsons (1904–5; reprint, New York: Charles Scribner's Sons, 1958), pp. 181–82.

bureaucratic mechanism compares with other organizations exactly as does the machine with the non-mechanical modes of production."[14]

The metaphor of the machine, as that of the cage, produces the sort of anxiety Weber surely desired. But we must not lose sight of the consequences such images entail. Bureaucracies become efficient, impersonal "entities" capable of running their programs as independent entities.[15] To use a more animate metaphor, they *take on lives of their own*. They must continue to achieve the objectives their constituents set for them in order to continue to receive support, and indeed we should expect them to achieve them at ever higher levels. But we should also expect that their methods will come less and less to resemble the day-to-day methods of the constituents who support them. Correspondingly, even their objectives come to be shaped by others on the "inside," others who benefit directly from the direction of the organization's programs.

Although no actual organization corresponds to this ideal-typical description, these sorts of charges were leveled at the SBC bureaucracy by fundamentalists and centrist-conservatives beginning in the early 1960s. As I recounted earlier, the Sunday School Board, the Home Mission Board, the Christian Life Commission, and the Baptist Joint Committee on Public Affairs came under special attack for failing to represent the wishes, or achieve the objectives, of the denomination. These organizations had become "things in themselves," promoting programs that were efficient but that did not meet the needs of most constituent Southern Baptists as those folks perceived them. The bureaucracy, the fundamentalists charged, had become an inner-circle of denominational elites.

Fundamentalists further charged that these elites were using the pressures at their disposal to ensure their continued self-perpetuation.[16] Specifically, they appointed allies to denominational posts and used their influence to recommend their friends to the best pulpits.[17]

Berger's description of the economic and political pressures involved with religious bureaucracy helps us here. A less-subtle reading of Weber might lead us to believe that because these organizations in the SBC were efficient

14. Max Weber, "Bureaucracy," in *From Max Weber*, p. 214.

15. I emphasize the term "entities" only because it has become a darling catchphrase in the SBC bureaucracy, perhaps pointing once again to the "new" institutionalism now in vogue.

16. Said a fundamentalist leader, "Generally speaking, when you get a big bureaucracy the most important thing about it is to perpetuate itself."

17. No fundamentalist leaders have told us they wanted denominational power. Nearly every one mentioned resentfully that it seemed odd that men in pastorates as large and influential as theirs had never been asked to participate.

and because they intended to perpetuate themselves, they would continue to do so. But Berger points out the other side of the coin: such efficiency does not lead to self-perpetuation if the organization is not *perceived* as meeting the objectives the group has set for it.

Weber first noted that democracy and bureaucracy had an ambiguous relationship: "democracy has to promote what reason demands and democratic sentiment hates."[18] The two, the centralizing tendency toward efficiency and the democratic desire to disperse power, are held in balance. In this case, Fundamentalists were able to establish, to the satisfaction of a majority of messengers, that the scales needed to be tipped toward a dispersal of power, at least toward a rejection of those currently on the inside.

Once they had done so, however, fundamentalists found that being the "new" insiders required a greater attention to bureaucratic imperatives than some had realized. The organizations they had commandeered truly *were* efficient in many ways. Although a change in leadership was rapidly accomplished, it became quickly apparent that much of the structure was as it was for a very good reason. Wholesale changes might satisfy their constituents' demands for a direction more consistent with the majority's beliefs, but inefficiency would quickly come to be regarded as failure.

The Virtue, and Limits, of Compromise

The result, as we might expect, has been a sort of compromise, a new balance, between new fundamentalist objectives and the old organizational machinery. Harrison predicted of American Baptists:

> In fact, by means of a representational system which fails to represent a shamefully large sector of the denomination the Baptists have made efforts to curtail all dissenting voices. In part, the excuse has been rooted in an experience of recent decades with a vocal minority which is bent on *destroying the values of denominational organization. But it has been shown that, in all probability, even if the fundamentalists were to gain control of the national organization, they would find it necessary to be obedient to the organizational imperatives if they wished to remain in power.* (Emphasis added.)[19]

18. Geerth and Mills's introduction to *From Max Weber*, p. 18.
19. Harrison, *Authority and Power*, p. 223.

Fundamentalists have attempted to change the rules for membership in the bureaucracy following much the same biblical guidelines used in the Convention as a whole.[20] Beyond that, however, fundamentalists have not found it necessary to make wholesale changes in the denomination's programs or policies.[21] As is so often the case in secular politics, their ideological and rhetorical purity did not translate easily into new programs that would be both more "correct" and more "pure" than the old.

The difficulty in translating such purity into practical application suggests a second "problem" and a corresponding compromise. While there may have been an identifiable fundamentalist ideology around which the key leaders rallied, the leaders themselves were men of great influence and conviction. Most of them were accustomed to being the top, if not absolute, authority in their local congregations. Those who were not pastors were leaders in some other capacity. Although these men banded together for a common purpose, they were unlikely to be confined by any one interpretation of the practical implications their ideology suggested.

Given that, those who emerged as leaders—the new bureaucratic leaders in particular—had their own ideas and their own managerial styles. They may have agreed with other fundamentalist leaders about the new biblical parameters, but they were unlikely to be in full agreement about programs or policies. They found, moreover, that the staff members already in place (and even some of the "moderate" board members) knew their jobs well and did not even differ theologically to the degree all the rhetoric might have led one to expect. In short, the fundamentalists often found that the bureaucracies were efficient organizations staffed by real, normal people. The new leaders were themselves real people usually willing to work with others within the new limits.[22]

These two kinds of compromises—new leaders dealing with existing structures, and pure ideology assuming practical, human applications—did not

20. It remains to be seen what the "membership" status of women will be, though events at the Home Mission Board make it apparent that ordained women will not be welcome.
21. When I asked Larry Lewis, the then new fundamentalist president of the Home Mission Board, what had changed since he arrived, he cited (1) a more stringent interview process, which includes screening for proper doctrine, and (2) a more hierarchical bureaucratic structure in which he is more directly involved in hiring and policy practices. These two are directly consistent with the claim that the denomination has chosen to reemphasize biblical parameters and pastoral authority.
22. More than one "moderate" staffer recounted to researchers at the Center for Religious Research that the changes at the Home Mission Board were toward greater efficiency with less intolerance than they had expected.

suit everybody. Some on the far right of the denomination were unhappy with the lack of ideological purity.[23] Those farthest to the left were unhappy with the new leadership, but more often than not because they were unhappy with the new parameters for membership.[24] They have also charged that the new bureaucracy and the new trustees were chosen to toe a strict ideological line. Whether or not they were chosen for that reason no one (but those in the nominating process) can say; that such a vivid line exists has become increasingly unclear.[25]

The third kind of compromise stems from the other two. Not only must the new leaders compromise with the established structures and the ideology be compromised by practical necessity, but bureaucracy itself is always in tension with the democratic structures it represents. That democracy is premised on what I have called a "rough spiritual equality," what Weber calls the "equal rights of the governed."[26] Such democracy, Weber says, includes these postulates:

(1) Prevention of the development of a closed status group of officials in the interest of a universal accessibility of office and

(2) minimization of the authority of officialdom in the interest of expanding the sphere of influence of "public opinion" as far as practicable.[27]

Thus democracy always seeks to *prevent* the entrenchment of leaders and the development of expertise that cannot be duplicated, even while it requires bureaucracy that seeks exactly those goals. The two—democracy and the bureaucracy it creates—are thus held in irresolvable tension. Ideally, the bureaucracy performs with the precision and efficiency required, and the democracy serves to check its growth and independence. The events within

23. The story of the BJCPA and the Religious Liberty Commission is the best example of this reaction.

24. There have been some serious concerns. Moderates charge that fundamentalists want to deemphasize Foreign Missions and to place political, social concerns over personal evangelism. However, such charges have given off more heat than light.

25. The moderate charge most often repeated is that the central network of fundamentalist leaders responds to the direction of their political organizers, Pressler and Patterson. That these two have indeed been at the heart of the denomination's transformation is undeniable; that there is a leader-group of elites is equally clear. That the new bureaucratic leaders are uniformly guided, or beholden, to this group is unlikely (indeed preposterous), as other events have demonstrated.

26. Weber, "Bureaucracy," in *From Max Weber*, p. 226.

27. Ibid.

the Southern Baptist Convention in the past fourteen years can be interpreted in just such a light. The bureaucracy had developed an internal elite, insufficiently connected to the majority denomination's constituents. These constituents applied democratic pressure for changes in the organization, specifically for changes within the elite group of leaders, but still find that they need these organizations in precisely the capacities for which they were developed.

In this way, democracy "worked" in the SBC. Those accepted as full members exercised their rights in the most direct way possible: they voted out an old establishment, pruning back the growth of an independent bureaucracy. All of the Convention, including the bureaucratic elites, were forced to admit that the fundamentalists and other conservatives fell under the umbrella of membership and therefore had a right to vote as they wanted to (even if they did not imagine such folks would ever muster a majority). However, the current "establishment," the fundamentalists, will surely be constrained by the *rights* and the voting privileges of those who are still considered members even under the new, "informal," biblical guidelines.

Such claims—that fundamentalists must negotiate both in the arena of organizational efficiency and in the arena of democratic group governance— cannot be left at the level of abstract or ideal-typical analysis. Recent events in the SBC support these contentions, while simultaneously offering caveats about predicting the future based only on the events and specific program changes of the recent past.

One example, albeit tenuous, of compromise or negotiation is the failure of the proposed Religious Liberty Commission. Chapter 2 described the events surrounding the proposal and the debate concerning this new commission. The Las Vegas annual meeting was a "showdown" in which the limits of the fundamentalist coalition, if any, would be exposed.

Those weaknesses were indeed exposed, but the fundamentalists demonstrated a new kind of strength at the same time. On the opening day of the convention, Vines won the customary second term by a margin of approximately 10 percent against the moderates' conservative candidate, Daniel Vestal. That Vestal was both an inerrantist and a member of Southern Baptists Committed reinforces my claims that the guidelines for candidate selection have now been set and that the Southern Baptists Committed are the true opposition party now. The budget proposed by the Executive Committee passed easily. Everything seemed on an even, conciliatory keel.

However, a motion from the floor to defund the BJCPA, coming after the motion of the Religious Liberty Commission had been postponed, broke the harmony of the meeting.[28] That motion required a further motion to "reconsider" the budget. Although the Executive Committee had intentionally moved to avoid sponsoring such a controversy, the controversy arose just the same.[29]

The motion to "reconsider" received sustained debate. Frank Ingraham, a moderate Executive Committee member who had praised Vines's peacekeeping attempt, spoke against the motion. He said that these matters were complex and that the Committee had considered them in good and proper order. Fundamentalist leader Adrian Rogers spoke for reconsideration. He stated that he "had been around this mountain enough" and wanted to settle the matter by vote once and for all.

Rogers's desire for clarity came conveniently after fundamentalists knew the results of the presidential vote.[30] The convention that had elected Vines by a wide margin would now vote again on the fate of the BJCPA. Many fundamentalists doubtless hoped that this time they had a majority in place. But it was not to be. Even though embattled BJCPA Chairman James Dunn was not allowed to speak until *after* the vote to reconsider (albeit before the actual "up or down" vote on his funding, should the motion to reconsider pass), the motion failed by about the same 10 percent margin Vines had enjoyed.[31]

This margin proved that the decision to defer Executive Committee recommendation of the RLC was a fortunate one for fundamentalists. It suggested that a current string of fundamentalist presidents did not mean unrestrained authority for any political party, group of leaders, or ideology. The same democratic mechanisms that made the current bureaucratic changes

28. Actually, there were two motions. The first was to defund the BJCPA and give the money to Southeastern Seminary. When Lewis Drummond, as new Southeastern president, rejected such a request, the messenger deferred to a motion by Kenneth Barnett of Colorado to defund the BJCPA and give the money to the HMB, the FMB, the CLC and the PAC.

29. The fact that the Executive Committee did not sponsor such a change does not mean there was not a concerted fundamentalist effort to do so anyway. Thomas Pratt, fundamentalist head of the PAC, told me to expect activity from the floor on the issue. It cannot be coincidental that Kenneth Barnett, a close friend of Pratt's, made the motion to defund.

30. In a face-to-face "discussion," a young messenger accused Rogers of intentionally waiting until the fundamentalists could expect a majority before moving to reconsider the budget. Why, the messenger asked, was the budget not reconsidered when first presented?

31. While that margin is substantial, my reading of the situation is that an actual "up or down" vote would have produced an even wider margin. Some probably voted to settle the matter—following advice of Rogers, who would have voted with the BJCPA to settle it. The flip side of such arguments is that the denominational loyalists who voted to support the Executive Committee's actions on the budget, and so voted against the motion to reconsider, might also have voted with the Executive Committee had the RLC been proposed.

possible could also make other proposed changes impossible, at least until sufficient numbers of moderates ceased their participation. Fundamentalists did not have a monolithic hold on the Convention, they simply had the sympathies of the majority in their bid to set biblical parameters for membership. Movement beyond that, especially into secular, political areas, appeared subject to limitation by the Convention.[32]

The RLC proposal passed away quietly. That fact alone supports earlier arguments that pure ideology must be compromised when human agents seek to institutionalize it. Both Larry Lewis and Richard Land are fundamentalists who came into the bureaucracy with the support of the coalition of fundamentalist leaders who have organized their allies for the past ten elections. Neither, however, seemed hesitant to reject the idea of the new RLC despite Judge Pressler's vocal support for it. They have specific responsibilities, both to their particular institutions and as stewards of the denomination's resources, that compel them to speak out when they believe money is being allocated inappropriately or programs are pursued unwisely. That they challenged this proposal speaks volumes for the power of institutional prerogatives and for the "centering" effects of bureaucracy and democracy.[33]

But specific challenges within the coalition did not mean the larger goal could not be accomplished. In 1990 the messengers in New Orleans voted to cut BJCPA funding from $400,000 back to $50,000. In 1991 in Atlanta they voted to withdraw funding altogether. Program responsibilities concerning religious freedom would now rest with Richard Land and the Christian Life Commission. As moderates withdrew from active involvement in the annual meetings, fundamentalist objectives became easier to reach, in spite of internal difference of opinion.

As has often been remarked concerning the American national government, bureaucratic and democratic pressure move politicians—especially presidents—toward the political center despite their past rhetoric. The more varied one's constituency is, the more likely one is to develop a centrist, pragmatic approach. I contend that we have seen something of that process in the SBC, but we have also seen a narrowing of the constituency for which

32. This is not to suggest either that the BJCPA or other, direct SBC agencies were not already involved in secular politics. It is only to say that the "new" changes in the SBC did not automatically or necessarily extend to all possible areas.

33. Darrell Robinson, then vice-president of the Executive Committee, sided with Land in opposing the RLC even though he was rumored to be the next head of the powerful Executive Committee. (He later resigned from the Executive Committee to take a leadership post elsewhere in the bureaucracy.)

there is no neat civil parallel. Fundamentalists have been able to open up the processes in certain internal ways as they simultaneously succeeded in closing the ranks of membership.

One signal of this opening was the nomination and election, in 1989 in Las Vegas, of Richard Jackson to be a trustee of the Home Mission Board. The nomination of Jackson, the losing "moderate" presidential candidate in both 1987 and 1988 (he lost by less than 1 percent in 1988), marked the first time that an actual opposition candidate had been selected for such an important post within the denomination.

Some might protest that the nomination does not constitute compromise because Jackson is a strict inerrantist. He is, of course, and that only reinforces the argument being advanced in Chapters 5 and 6. Jackson is, by every conceivable standard of measurement, a "member" of the Southern Baptist Convention. His church is a leader, often *the* leader, in the denomination in both baptisms and Cooperative Program giving. His own extraordinary evangelistic skills make him a natural for the Home Mission Board.

But he is not a member of the fundamentalist coalition—indeed, he is one of its most outspoken critics.[34] Putting Jackson on the Home Mission Board suggested that fundamentalist leaders had taken to heart his complaints about being "excluded," both personally and as part of the large group of "outsiders." Though many of the fundamentalists I spoke with did not want to interpret this action as a symbol of major importance, such a conclusion is difficult to escape.[35] The coalition recognized Jackson as someone from the "opposition party" who is still a member of the denomination. His nomination and election seem to indicate that the fundamentalists were willing to reach beyond their own group of elites to include others they consider members.[36]

Even if one were to suggest cynically, as such political scenes seem to

34. I have already recounted the verbal exchange between Jackson and Judge Pressler at the Executive Committee meeting in Nashville in February 1989. When Jackson gave the nominating speech for moderate candidate Winfred Moore in 1986 in Atlanta, one fundamentalist Convention president told me that Jackson had "disappointed" a lot of people and proven himself not to be the "friend" some had thought he was.

35. Paige Patterson described the nomination as a way of reaching out to "Richard" personally, one way "we could show him that we love and appreciate him as a brother." Conservative journalist James Hefley credited the move to the pragmatism of Larry Lewis, who was himself pleased to announce the news to me as a "scoop."

36. It is fair to say that the old establishment did the same. However, that group did not consider fundamentalists to be "full" members any more than fundamentalists accord that privilege to them. While both grant the other certain statutory rights, neither admits full participation by the other when they have the institutional power to prevent it.

require, that the fundamentalists hoped only to co-opt or hush Jackson, the result is still the same. The coalition was learning to "play ball" with the other team out of political necessity, even as it narrowed the range of opposition players.

One fundamentalist leader who spoke proudly of Jackson's nomination was willing to call the event symbolic. It signaled, the leader believed, a recognition on the part of the coalition that they had "won" in setting the new parameters and that they now needed—for both ethical and political reasons—to reach out to others who fell within those parameters but who had not thrown their lot in with the coalition. In the future, he proposed, we might see candidates chosen not *because* they had the proper battle scars but precisely because they lacked them. It was perhaps time to tone down the political rhetoric and emphasize the themes—such as soul-winning—with which no Baptists (including the opposition party) could publicly disagree.

Many in the denomination were stinging from the heated rhetoric and institutional upheaval of the last decade and were seeking some peace and stability in the future. Perhaps that is the reason they rejected the potential controversies and embraced the "soul-winning" theme of the Las Vegas meeting so readily. Fundamentalists had now to realize that the antiestablishment sentiment that swept them in could be used against them. Most Baptists recognized the rights of others to vote, to voice opinions, and to serve. Fundamentalists needed to recognize those rights too—at least for those within the new parameters—or risk losing their new status as leaders.

They needed to recognize too that their support during the last ten years did not signal total agreement with every policy a coalition member might recommend. The denomination apparently agreed with them about the need for biblical guidance and pastoral authority, but this did not necessarily translate into support for particular programs. For political reasons, men such as Jerry Vines were going to be forced to choose, in his words, the "best people possible" for job openings as long as they fell within the new interpretation of the Baptist Faith and Message. What had once been construed as an excuse for choosing only coalition supporters was now going to be a more realistic guide for returning democratic governance to the larger body.

Both the democratic and bureaucratic changes in the SBC indicate that those mechanisms are alive and functioning, if not exactly "well." They are not "well" because the denomination's polity was created not to harbor a "competing interest" model of democracy with established, contending parties but to institutionalize consensus. Although there is a new biblical consensus—what has here been called "loose inerrancy"—it was purchased at the price of a hostile two-party system in which one party was simply ousted from contention. The SBC will need to develop mechanisms for institution-alizing the changes it has in fact already undergone.

Such institutionalization requires that Southern Baptists address issues of dissent and avenues for change within the newly defined "parameters" for membership. In the recent crisis of pluralism, members turned to democratic and procedural mechanisms that rang true to their experiences as Baptists and Americans. Those mechanisms saw them through, but not without a great expense of energy and a loss of goodwill. As the dust settles, it would be prudent to reflect on the theological and organizational roots of the con-troversy and to ask what it says about the future of the SBC and about denominations more generally.

7

The New Southern Baptist Democracies

The New Official Polity

The SBC has now regained a certain calm, having in many ways redrawn the lines of membership. Those attending the annual meeting in Atlanta in 1991 were usually of one voice; former moderate leaders, for the most part, avoided the annual meeting, attending instead a meeting of the new Cooperative Baptist Fellowship (CBF), also in Atlanta in 1991. The future denominational affiliation of the CBF is uncertain. More certain, however, is the claim that the moderates now separating themselves from the "official" SBC are unlikely to be full members again.

Looking back at the controversy in the denomination, one can now ask, "What happened?" One answer is that the SBC lacked sufficient mechanisms for institutionalizing dissent, so it both enraged—and ultimately politicized—a biblically conservative majority and later ostracized the highly committed minority that once formed the denomination's establishment. Again we may return to Harrison as he chastised the American Baptists:

> One of the problems never adequately faced by the Baptists is the adequate institutionalization or legitimation of dissident groups

within the denominational structure. The fundamentalists are justifiably considered a threat to the stability of the denominational structure but little is gained by pushing them aside and awaiting the day
when they shall gain sufficient power to reverse the procedure. In the
world of secular politics the rights of the opposition are preserved
through such institutions as the party system, minority rights and
civil liberties. It is a strong indictment against the Baptists that they
have not discovered any means to permit their own minorities a voice
in the convention. In fact, by means of a representational system
which fails to represent a shamefully large sector of the denomination, the Baptists have made efforts to curtail all dissenting voices.[1]

Harrison was, of course, speaking to the "moderate" establishment in the
American Baptist Churches in the 1950s. His warning could just as easily
have been aimed at the SBC establishment in the 1960s and 1970s. Obvi-
ously, fundamentalists within the SBC did "gain sufficient power" and did
"reverse the procedure." Their actions proved Harrison's indictment accurate.

But that could hardly be considered the end of the story. Insofar as the
fundamentalists have *"reversed"* the procedure, they risk putting themselves
under the same judgment they visited on the old, moderate establishment.
Should they fail to institutionalize dissent efficiently, they could find themselves—perhaps far in the future—in another struggle for power. In an organization like the SBC, those in power must always respect the wishes of their
constituency to check that power, whether with claims of biblical accuracy
or individual autonomy. The history of the SBC is the history of the growth
of a central bureaucracy and of the constant populist will to check it. It
would be rash to assume that the recent "revolution" could be immune to
the same impulses that created it. The luxury of patience was once accorded
the moderate establishment because it was so painful for Southern Baptists
to admit that their bureaucracy no longer adequately represented their interests. It was difficult to face the fact that the old consensus was gone and that
there was palpable, genuine disagreement between people who had less in
common than they thought.[2] The Convention was hesitant to articulate

1. Harrison, *Authority and Power*, p. 223.
2. I do not deny that, when compared to American society as a whole, Southern Baptists
can look pretty similar. Nonetheless, differences in class, education, level of urbanization, and
a myriad of other factors support my claims of dissimilarity, a fact that is magnified by their
supposed common cultural heritage. Painting the Southern Baptists with too broad a brush
can only cause one to miss the significance and the sources of their disagreements, as Ellen
Rosenberg does in her *Southern Baptists: A Subculture in Transition*.

more fixed parameters for membership or to institutionalize what I have called a competing-interest model of denominational polity.

Circumstances forced them to do both. While some Southern Baptists might still say that there are no doctrinal requirements for membership, it is clear to all that the inerrantist interpretation of the Baptist Faith and Message now serves as the guideline for full participation in the denomination.[3] The presidential votes of the last few years make it even more clear that the Convention developed, and then discarded, a two-party system. Although that system has probably disappeared with the exodus of moderate leaders, the potential for overtly political resolution of problems within the polity remains.

The cat is out of the bag, so to speak, and cannot be put back inside. If the current bureaucracy is unresponsive to the desires of the messengers, or if the members of the new leadership elite are perceived as unfair, the Convention will not find it nearly so difficult to make changes the second time. The fundamentalists found that the old system was unresponsive to their dissenting voices but that, because of its antiquated methods for selecting messengers, it was ripe for exploitation. Unable (and in many cases unwilling) to change those methods, however, fundamentalists now find themselves potentially subject to the same pressures they were able to apply.

This is not to say that a new coup is on the horizon. There was palpable harmony at the 1991 meeting. The sitting president was reelected unanimously. The sitting recording secretary—a moderate—was reelected, despite obvious efforts by some in the coalition to unseat him. There was little incivility toward—indeed, little mention of—moderates who had chosen to attend a different meeting.

That civility notwithstanding, the SBC can never forget that it holds within itself the seeds of party politics, of a forum for competing interests. If the interests of the newly limited membership seem once again harmonious, who can say what problems pluralism may present in the future.[4]

3. The first and last word on the Baptist Faith and Message is Herschel Hobbs, of the committee that originally drafted it. His *What Baptists Believe* (Nashville, Tenn.: Broadman Press, 1964) gives the "traditional" (1964) Baptist reading of the document as it was drafted. Hobbs is now cited by both sides as supporting their views. While there can be little doubt that Hobbs is himself a very conservative biblicist interested in making peace in the denomination, both sides still identify him with the "old establishment" when they attempt to claim his views as their own.

4. One of the largest SBC congregations in the Midwest, with more than ten full-time staff members, sent no one from the staff as a messenger in 1992. One associate pastor said, "I expect they'll come after those of us in the spiritual renewal (a group with charismatic overtones) movement next."

The Institutionalization of Dissent

Will the SBC move to counteract future conflict by "reaching out" or "open-ing up"? In what concrete ways could the Convention move to institution-alize and legitimize dissent? Allowing time for an opposition candidate for president to speak is one such step. While this presents various potential problems—the "parties" were never officially recognized, so there was no way to say who the "official" candidates were—such an official forum for disagree-ment seems prudent in the future. When there are multiple nominations, perhaps messengers could vote on two or three whom they choose to hear speak. However the details of such a change are established, the Convention asserted its will, in Las Vegas, to move in this direction. If it forgets institu-tional steps such as these now that the furor has subsided, it does so at its own peril.

Another possible change is the recognition of substitutions or deletions in the nominating process. There has already been substantial debate about this matter, but more is likely to come. The Convention has been sensitized, almost against its will, to the potential for abuse in the current system. Not only those in any future opposition group, but also those in the large middle, are likely to be more vigilant about this process in the future.

In Las Vegas there was yet another motion from the floor to review the possibility of holding the annual meeting in multiple cities through the use of closed-circuit television.[5] That proposal again met stiff opposition, osten-sibly for technical and financial reasons, but it did not go away. The neces-sary technology and its attendant costs seem mind-boggling, but no more so than conventions with 40,000-plus messengers, closed-circuit television in one building, and an electronic system for distributing opportunities for mes-sengers to speak would have seemed ten years ago. Furthermore, the meet-ings may now be seen nationally on Baptist Television Network (BTN) cable. The Convention has shown that it is willing to spend the money and to exploit the necessary technology to serve the interests of fairness in the re-cent past. One can expect that they will continue to do so in the future, although a motion to distribute ballots to all churches in the denomination was soundly, and nearly unanimously, defeated in Atlanta in 1991.

Conventions held in multiple cities would indeed test the limits of the

5. There were also similar motions to provide voting opportunities for churches unable to attend the Convention and to provide scholarships and/or housing for those who might be financially unable to attend. See *SBC Annual, 1989*, esp. pp. 38, 46.

current polity. The potential of such a system is unclear. Would an increase in opportunities for the poorer, more rural churches strengthen the fundamentalists?[6] Or would this broadening undercut the organizational advantages the fundamentalists already enjoy?[7] Answers to those questions will require empirical research if and when the time comes. For the present, we should expect the issue of "opening" the convention meetings to as many messengers as possible to continue to recur—less emotionally, but persistently.

The details of these structural changes are not as important as the necessities they represent. Those necessities will be addressed with *informal* ways to legitimize dissent that will determine the shape of the more formal, institutional ways. The nomination and election of Richard Jackson to the Home Mission Board suggests one such informal way. The choice of presidential candidates who have *not* been in the denominational wars, if such choices are made in the future, will be yet another. The eventual defeat of the BJCPA is a counter-example. Meetings in New Orleans in 1990 and Atlanta in 1991 signaled an end to the controversy but showed few signs of organizational revision.

One method that will not be seriously discussed, however, is a system that is more truly representational. For all of his prescience, Harrison's recommendations, when applied to Southern Baptists, fall short on this point. True representation is a pill Southern Baptists are unlikely to swallow. Harrison recommended to American Baptists that they take their membership in associations more seriously; in essence, associations should be treated as congressional districts or wards. There could be open debate within these, and then representatives (not messengers) would carry the authority of their association to the Convention. Correspondingly, they would carry the authority of the Convention back to the associations. Decisions would be binding because they were legitimated by the votes of duly elected representatives.[8]

Harrison's point is well taken. If there is, after all, going to be a large bureaucracy with a great deal of power and ostensibly guided by the votes of the members, why not make those votes represent the whole membership as

6. The obvious answer seems to be yes, though the fundamentalists are most opposed to this idea.

7. Key leaders in the fundamentalist coalition have repeatedly denied the charge that they ever chartered any buses. Any such activities, which are nearly impossible to document, were undertaken by individual churches or associations.

8. Harrison, *Authority and Power*, chap. 5.

accurately as possible? If the bureaucracy is perceived to speak and act for the membership and to spend its money, why not officially recognize that representation? The power of the bureaucrats to decide, as Harrison points out, already exists in fact and is not diminished simply because Baptists are reluctant to admit this.[9] Why not acknowledge "official" channels for delegating this power and authority that could, at the same time, serve to limit both, precisely because such channels both prescribe and proscribe appropriate activity?

The answer to those questions is now obvious. Southern Baptists are unwilling to establish such formal channels for power and authority because they are committed in theory to individual liberty and committed in fact to the authority of scripture and of pastoral leadership, both of which would be threatened by acknowledging the official power of a Baptist hierarchy. It is not that they disproved Harrison's contention; indeed, the SBC is an excellent example of the problems that arise when power is not limited by acknowledged authority. They have shown, instead, that the structures of power and authority are too complex to be contained by any one polity or organizational arrangement. Democratic, political models were the most efficient mechanism for dealing with problems on a large organizational scale, but the give-and-take of daily life would happen at many different levels of experience, using different models of and for action. The SBC has developed a large bureaucracy to handle its various programs and has different organizational models in the local congregations. The types of authority or power present in these must be included in a serious conversation about the future of the denomination.

A mixture of democracy, bureaucracy, charisma, scriptural legalism, populist sentiment, and individual autonomy is necessary for the denomination—as for the American state—to realign and rebalance itself in times of conflict or discord. Some of these trends may be identified with what Weber termed "rational-legal"—indeed, much of what appears to be "church-like" organization fits this pattern.

But there are other tendencies that must be figured into the equation. Both tradition and charisma seem strangely irrational, but experience teaches us that they do not disappear from history. These impulses—along with participatory democracy—have been loosely identified with more sectarian organizational forms. In the SBC a combination of these trends is

9. Says Harrison (ibid., p. 216), "The presence of power is not eliminated by noble intentions."

working together, using models borrowed from the secular political environment, to create a uniquely American denomination.

The Institutional Complexity of Modern Life

Southern Baptists, as the rest of us, relate to a complex world in a variety of ways. Certain ways of behaving or choosing "feel" right in a given situation. For Southern Baptists, as we might expect for others, decisions in the marketplace call for a cost-benefit analysis that all would recognize as inappropriate in the context of, say, parental discipline. Personal relationships in the workplace call for a more distanced, therapeutic approach than relationships at home or at church. Problems at church are often settled by appeal to specific biblical injunctions, while problems at home call for a broader code of general moral obligation.[10]

Such distinctions should not be surprising. Each of us operates on several planes of moral experience and bases decision-making on our perception of the "appropriateness" of an action to its context. Our lives have institutional contexts; we recognize actions that "belong" within the context of the economy, the polity, the family, and so on. Our organizations are particular groupings, with defined boundaries, that draw from any or all these institutional sources.

Southern Baptists must draw from these many different sources, even if their rhetoric suggests that they appeal only, or primarily, to the Bible for all moral guidance.[11] "Biblical" guidance is more likely to be consciously acknowledged in matters directly pertaining to the church; moreover, it should not seem odd that even "church" matters themselves present different subcontexts. For Southern Baptists, the "church" context for an action

10. All these generalizations come from my paper "The Relationship of Belief to Institutional Location," in which I argue that the moral actions of Southern Baptists are controlled by their context—there are appropriate (and different) ways to work at work, church, and home—despite their claims to be more "biblically based." The idea for studying this "moral complexity" comes directly from Steven Tipton's paper "Social Differentiation and Moral Pluralism," in which he sketches the concept of different styles of moral reasoning that are appropriate to different institutional contexts.

11. I certainly do not want to claim that Baptists do not appeal more to the Bible than some others. They do, of course, but it does not follow that they use the Bible as a guidebook for every situation. I found that specific biblical injunctions were used to justify actions only in the context of church-related moral crises.

could be a deacons' meeting, a worship service, an associational meeting, or an annual convention. Although certain "church-like" modes of thinking would apply across the range of these possibilities, there are differences— some subtle and some striking—between these, and Southern Baptists acknowledge those differences in their actions.

Denominations are ambiguous religious organizations. Denominations, including the SBC, are pragmatic, adjusting their actions to the appropriate context, whether congregation, annual meeting, or bureaucracy.[12]

This matter need not seem too abstract or theoretical: Southern Baptists consider it appropriate to think and act differently at annual conventions than they act in their local congregations. There is, of course, a great deal of overlap between the two. Different perceptions of pastoral and scriptural and democratic authority take on different meanings when they are translated from the local pulpit to the convention podium. But there are distinct attributes of each subcontext that are crucial to the Convention's polity.

In the local church context, for instance, one usually has considerably *more* freedom to dissent from the policies of the whole Convention. Local pastors, such as Cecil Sherman or William Self, were able to take early and often radical stands against the fundamentalist advance because they had no fear for their jobs or their security. They could be ostracized from the workings of the larger body—indeed they were—but the Convention could not remove them from their jobs or undercut their prestige or authority.

The freedom of the local church to dissent from the policies of the Convention is often mirrored by an absence of freedom to dissent *within the local church*. Some Southern Baptist churches are very democratic, some are oligarchic, and some are virtually totalitarian. The fundamentalist churches that have challenged the policies of the SBC since the early 1970s do not necessarily have any corresponding mechanism for "challenge" within their own polities. Similarly, some moderate laypeople may find it much easier to criticize the fundamentalist "takeover" than to point out the disagreements they have with their own pastor.

This is so because charismatic, pastoral authority does not translate easily from the pulpit to the political podium. Adrian Rogers, Jerry Vines, and Richard Jackson surely carry much of their personal charisma with them

---

12. David Martin, "The Denomination," *British Journal of Sociology* 13 (1962), 6: "In the sphere of organization the denomination tends to be pragmatic. Of course, it is not completely pragmatic any more than it is completely free of special institutional claims. . . . But there are no *particular* forms of organization which are regarded as being in the unique possession of a Divine imprimatur" (emphasis in the original).

when they go to the podium at the annual conventions, but there they have nowhere near the persuasive power they have in their own closed environments. They take on, instead, the role of moral leader—not unlike the American plebiscitary presidency—and attempt to use their moral persuasiveness to maintain a coalition of party loyalists and independents large enough to constitute a ruling majority.[13] The larger group has too much invested in democratic mechanisms and too much diversity of biblical interpretation—among people accustomed to power and authority themselves— to let any one person's authority or power go unchecked. Moreover, that person must always satisfy both his own party and a sufficient number of "independents" whose support he requires.

The SBC as a whole must therefore accept a wider range of views and give to any particular leader a smaller degree of authority than the local church does. The informal means for ensuring "right" biblical interpretation and "correct" action are simply not available on such a broad numerical and geographic scale. In the local church, personal pressure serves as a control on doctrine and behavior; at the national level, only more formal mechanisms can accomplish this task.

What this means, although it may at first glance seem paradoxical, is that the SBC must have more "fixed" boundaries than the local church, although these will actually be less stringent than the informal ones in the local church. In the face of previously unthinkable diversity, the Convention was forced to establish known—if sometimes only weakly enforceable—parameters for acceptable belief and practice. It could not use peer pressure, it could not even ultimately use the personal charisma of the great orators, to ensure compliance. Its only recourse was to decide what was intolerable and to establish guidelines for tolerating the rest.

In such situations the actors involved have no choice but to turn to regular, fixed rules for maintaining those guidelines or parameters. This is the true sense in which the Convention has become "politicized." It may, of course, find itself more involved in secular politics than it was before,[14] but

13. This idea comes from John Meyer, who has analyzed the creation of western nation-states and their role in the world system. See esp. John Meyer and W. Richard Scott, *Organizational Environments: Ritual and Rationality* (Newberry Park, Calif.: Sage Publications, 1983).

14. Some members of the fundamentalist coalition are involved in other, more overtly political activities associated with the New Christian Right. Edward MacAteer, of Bellevue Baptist in Memphis, sits on the Religious Roundtable. Richard Lee, of Atlanta, served as a director when Jerry Falwell assumed control of the PTL club and led the fight to ban the showing of the movie *The Last Temptation of Christ*. Adrian Rogers and Charles Stanley have both been visible in the pro-life movement. Of course, moderate leaders are more likely to be

that is beside the point. The Convention has been forced to adopt political solutions to *internal* problems that were originally theological in nature. It has been forced to retain the more hierarchical, formal organizational qualities of a denomination while still emphasizing right doctrine and separation from other secular values.

If the group here described sounds ambiguous, something like a bureaucratized sect, then it may well provoke yet a further comparison with the American polity. Developing parties must jockey for position—just as the conservative Southern Baptists Committee retreated from more radical early moderate stances—and must appeal to independents in the Convention on whatever grounds are available and practical: charisma, tradition, fairness, biblical soundness, and so on. The contending actors found themselves in two distinct political parties with a large, unaffiliated (or weakly affiliated) middle. Disagreement became ever more public, centering on differences in theology and worldview. Some settlement was expected to come through a vote, because compromise or, even more to the point, a meeting of hearts and minds through the guidance of the Holy Spirit was simply no longer expected by everyone.

The politicization here described occurred in the larger Convention without ever significantly altering the polity of most local churches. They continued to be more or less democratic, more or less inerrantist, and more or less dependent on the charisma of their pastor. But their messengers, drawn into a geographically and demographically diverse body, were subject to formal rules and mechanisms that are both unnecessary and unworkable at the local, personal level.

That the corporate efforts of these different churches with different polities should come to be governed by political mechanisms should come as no real surprise. Wolfgang Schluchter states:

> A functionally differentiated society too must be integrated through the coordination of the social spheres. This is, however, a negative rather than a positive integration. The rules of coordination are not meant to establish a permanent rank order among the spheres, which would be legitimated through the "unity of a highest value or through a value system or value hierarchy." Rather, the rules are supposed to make it impossible "that the operations of a partial system lead to

---

associated with more moderate political causes, although they have been notably less visible (undoubtedly partly because of the media's fascination with the New Christian Right).

insoluble problems in another partial system." When difficulties arise, *the regulatory needs are satisfied by recourse to secular values, especially political ones.* (Emphasis added.)[15]

Schluchter is, of course, talking about a large social system and not about a particular institution. His basic claim is that older social forms, particularly medieval ones, were coordinated by a Christian worldview and that "membership in society depend[ed] on belonging to a political and religious association." "Modern society," he claims, "has broken that connection, since it is a society based on functional differentiation."[16] In short, what was once a hierarchy of values has now been broken into several different value spheres whose interrelationship and coordination is maintained on an ad hoc basis and is usually regulated by appeal to secular, political values.

It may seem absurd to try to use such a focus to understand the Southern Baptist Convention. After all, it is still a fairly homogeneous unit, and membership in it is still dependent on certain religious associations. Nonetheless, Schluchter's analysis points in the right direction, even if his interpretive scheme cannot be transferred wholesale onto the data presented here.

The SBC has undergone many substantive changes in the last 100 years. The current "moderates" and "fundamentalists" within it are not simply similar people with different ideas (although they are sometimes that) but often quite different people with very different demographic backgrounds. While it would be futile to argue that they are "differentiated" in the sense one reserves for institutions with separate functions, it seems empirically obvious that they lacked sufficient "value overlap" or "value consensus" to settle their differences by appeal to shared values. There is no longer anything "popular" in the populist consensus. In this sense they resemble, in a formal and structural way, differentiated institutions that have different rules, suitable for their different functional contexts. These groups within the Convention had different worldviews located in different institutions, which suited their different backgrounds and needs.

These differences created a strain within the Convention. It became increasingly difficult to harmonize or "coordinate," in Schluchter's terms, these very different idea and value constellations into a coherent whole.

15. Wolfgang Schluchter, "The Future of Religion," in *Religion and America,* ed. Mary Douglas and Steven Tipton (Boston: Beacon Press, 1982), p. 72. The passages Schluchter quotes are Nicholas Luhmann's words.
16. Ibid.

Policies and doctrines that made sense to one group offended the sensibilities of the other.

The Convention responded to this tension in two very different ways. First, it reduced the pressure by placing limits on "real" or "true" membership. It developed a more general consensus that excluded, either in fact or in practice, the elements farthest from the center that were likely to cause the greatest strain. This has already occurred on the denomination's left, and it could occur on the right as well.

Although this luxury is not always available to larger societies in fact, it usually is in principle. Anarchists and communists are seldom ousted from our society, but they are generally ignored or ridiculed.[17] Libertarians and state socialists fare better, because their ideas are treated more seriously and are occasionally incorporated in a modified form, but they are seldom considered serious political contenders. In American politics and in the SBC, real political power means real, full membership. Such membership means proximity to the center of whatever general value-consensus can be established.

Placing limits, acknowledged or unacknowledged, on diversity is an option available to the SBC for which there is no neat parallel in Schluchter's social analysis. The SBC's other response to the disorganizing pressure within it is, however, very similar to the argument Schluchter develops. Having drawn the parameters for true membership as closely as could reasonably be expected, the Convention was still faced with dissonance and disagreement. It has responded to that pressure with greater emphasis on fairness and justice and equality (broadly conceived) in its political mechanisms.

What we have witnessed in the Convention is, then, a stage in what may well be a cycle of separation and reintegration. From its inception in the mid-nineteenth century until the mid-twentieth century, the SBC fought off disorganizing pressures and developed into a coherent institution with a polity that was generally democratic. In that process, it developed also a professional bureaucracy that would be both more efficient than, and in tension with, its broadly democratic polity, which was itself becoming increasingly diverse. The mid- to late twentieth century has seen a process of correction by which the majority of the SBC's constituents have brought the denomination's bureaucracy and programs back toward a stated biblical consensus, challenging the true membership both of the denomination's elite and of those who had, in their diversity, strayed too far from the center.

17. They are also occasionally incarcerated, of course.

Will the next step in the process then be a sort of reintegration in which those who do fall under the new consensus are able to secure a new harmony and a return to the "old ways" of doing things? The answer is both yes and no.

There are good reasons to believe that the Convention will experience a new unity as it continues to weed out those who no longer fit within its parameters and to insist on its own "rule of law" for those who do belong there. The SBC has shown itself able to adapt to changing environments, often through developing more task-specific suborganizations and sufficiently generalizable group values at the same time. The SBC has proven itself to be pragmatically successful within certain boundaries.[18]

Here the most important of those boundaries are inerrantist biblical interpretations that are part of the denomination's fabric. Christianity as a world religious movement may continue to adapt beyond such culture-laden, conservative biblicism, but Southern Baptists will cease to be Southern Baptists without it.[19]

Insofar as what I have called the "new biblical consensus" for membership holds, then, both the regular political mechanisms we have observed and the denomination's ability to adapt and to control should provide a renewed denominational unity in the near future. It is possible that the Convention can return for a time to some semblance of its pre-1960s harmony, the "old ways" of doing things.

But that "yes" is always confronted by a resounding "no." Yes, the Convention may find renewed stability as the consensus solidifies, but that new consensus will never be the same as the old. Practices may become more regular and less controversial, but the cultural homogeneity the SBC once enjoyed can never be recreated.

The new consensus is based more on cognitive assent to certain textual parameters than on cultural or social similarities. That consensus may create a new unity in the near future, but it will be difficult to hold as the denominations' social base continues to become more and more diverse, especially in the South. The Convention seems to be in the process of adapting now,

18. This argument is borrowed loosely from ideas developed by Talcott Parsons in *The Social System* (Glencoe, Ill.: The Free Press, 1951) and in *Social Systems and the Evolution of Action Theory* (Glencoe, Ill.: The Free Press, 1977).

19. Some have already stopped being Southern Baptist, and others will follow suit. Benton Johnson makes an interesting point that, in the process of separation, often one part of the split pair does not proceed in the process of inclusion and is effectively orphaned. There is a sense in which such a movement has happened to those who find themselves outside the "new consensus" in the SBC. From Benton Johnson, "Modernity and Pluralism," in *Pushing the Faith: Proselytism and Civility in a Pluralistic World*, ed. Frederick Greenspahn and Martin E. Marty (New York: Crossroads Press, 1988).

its shared values moving from the realm of common experience to the more general abstract and legalistic "parameters." There is no reason to believe, however, that those parameters will not themselves come under fire, giving way to a new rubric for determining membership, which will itself be subject to reevaluation and reformulation.

If the future of the denomination depends on its ability to maintain its ideological imperatives whatever other adaptive or inclusive measures it takes, its ultimate viability depends on the acceptance of that ideology—biblical inerrantism—by a sufficiently wide segment of the population within the denomination's environment. If, on the other hand, the denomination's future depends on its ability to grow, to expand, and to execute its programs, then its viability depends more on the procedures it has developed for dealing with internal tension. If the tenuous balance between centralizing, church-like impulses and the requirements of broad-based, autonomous participation depend on some common bond, then that bond is for Southern Baptists forged either by sufficient agreement on the meaning of scripture or by the political give-and-take involved in continuously establishing and legitimating a polity. The success of the SBC thus seems to hinge on the success of inerrancy as a twenty-first-century ideology in America, its own ability to adapt through formal procedures for reaching agreement, or some combination of the two.

The Other Southern Baptist Democracy

In 1991 Atlanta held not one but two annual meetings. The regular convention of the SBC was large—around 23,000—by historical standards, but not by comparison to the meetings held during the heat of the controversy. The meeting was virtually "event"-free and was run with a very civil tone.

A few weeks earlier, an impressively large group of moderates—approximately 6,000—held a meeting at which they established organizational guidelines and elected officers for the fledgling Cooperative Baptist Fellowship. Although the press focused on the likelihood that this group was about to secede from the SBC—indeed, one UPI report on National Public Radio claimed that it had done so—secession was only one issue on the minds of the delegates (and, in fact, they did not decide to withdraw at that time). Also pressing were the issues of polity and cooperation in the new group; no one in this assembly, drawn from the most liberal Southern Baptists and the displaced former establishment, needed to be reminded of the importance of such details in the development of new organizations.

It is not surprising that the group chose to incorporate structures they hoped would increase the accountability of moderators, board members, and other leaders. They elected women as well as men, frequently choosing from among those who had not been leaders in the old SBC (although many of those former leaders were present and have assumed some sort of leadership role). They devoted part of their budget to support of the BJCPA.

More surprising was the insistence that this was not simply another, new denomination, but by their account a cooperative effort of individual congregations, all of which still also cooperated with the SBC at least nominally, with the goal of providing new and different opportunities for social and mission work. Even Ammerman, having joined the fray once her research on the SBC was completed and published,[20] maintained that this was to be a new sort of reality in American religious organization.

The history of American religions makes one cautious about any such claims, but this much is clear: moderates in the SBC now have the organizational structures needed to separate themselves—either formally or in practice—from the new leadership in the SBC. We might expect that many—perhaps as many as 500,000 to 1,000,000—will do so, but we must remember that even those large numbers are a small fraction of the 15,000,000 members the SBC now claims.

As the futures of these two organizations unfold, the same sorts of polity questions can be posed to both. Will the Cooperative Baptist Fellowship be able to institute a nonhierarchical polity that emphasizes participation over doctrinal bounds for membership? If it does, will it be able to maintain the ideological imperatives necessary for growth? Similarly, if the Southern Baptist Convention continues to emphasize highly doctrinal limits on participation, will it continue to find receptive audiences, and new members, who can fit within the "parameters"?

A precarious balance of ideological commitment and flexible standards for membership and participation made the SBC the nation's largest Protestant denomination.[21] It is not yet clear what will result from the efforts of reformers who tamper with either side of the balance.

20. As in Ammerman's *Baptist Battles*. I believe, and reviews by other scholars as well as by Southern Baptists on both sides of the battle confirm, that this is the most sociologically complete and accurate description of the SBC.

21. John Scalf, Michael Miller, and Charles Thomas ("Goal Specificity, Organizational Structure, and Participant Commitment in Churches," *Sociological Analysis* 34 [Fall 1973], 169–84) noted that ideological commitment, formal rules, and rigid organizational structure are usually associated with the traditional ideology we think of as sectarian. That is, it is not necessarily the case that liberal "churches" are more organized and that "conservative" sects are less so.

8

Lessons For and About
Denominations

Specific History and General Theory

It would be easy to look back at the turmoil in the Southern Baptist Convention as a historical blip. Perhaps this was an isolated case. Perhaps the trou-
bles in the SBC resulted from a particular combination of practices, beliefs,
socioeconomic classes, and region that is unlikely to be reproduced elsewhere. If that is so, then neither Southern Baptists nor others need to spend
too much time recounting the crisis. For Southern Baptists there can be
some sense of closure; for others, there is a sense of safe distance.

Some elements of this history, as with any particular history, are unique.
There is no other denomination exactly like the Southern Baptist Convention. Nonetheless, this history must be recounted and interpreted precisely
because the SBC embodies elements common to most other American denominations. If there is such a thing as the "denominational type"—and I
believe there is good reason to make such a designation—then it is important
to understand which pieces of the Southern Baptist controversy stem from
circumstances that are uniquely Southern Baptist and which pieces stem
from that type of religious organization.

Two separate kinds of lessons can be learned. Southern Baptists must appropriate their history in order to approach their future. They must ask: What were the causes of the controversy? What issues were at stake? Why did the foment bubble over when and where it did?

The point is not, of course, that Southern Baptists must learn these things in order to avoid future controversies no matter what. Nothing inherent in Christian ecclesiology says that unity must be maintained at all costs. The point is that only now, after the dust has settled, is it possible to look back and fully appreciate what was gained and what was lost. Were the intended goals achieved? Were the unintended consequences worth the cost? Southern Baptists must answer these questions for themselves as they sift through the emerging literature about the crisis.

The other kind of lesson to be learned is much broader. Other denominations must try to decide how much of the SBC's controversy was rooted in that denomination's unique attributes—southern, congregational, conservative—and how much of it comes from the fluid, individualistic nature of the denominational type common to them all. Disgruntled conservatives in the SBC used explicitly political means to achieve ecclesiological change. If that sort of activity is possible in other large religious groups, then perhaps there is a deeper relationship between secular politics and denominations with very broad consequences for both.

How the Controversy Is Uniquely Southern Baptist

The controversy is uniquely Southern Baptist first because the SBC is uniquely southern. Although it is wise not to overgeneralize about southern culture, our common sense that the term "the South" means something is probably well placed. One thing "southern" or "the South" means is a kind of populism once proclaimed in such terms as "state's rights." The coincidence between southern political individualism, southern evangelicalism, and Southern Baptist polity is no coincidence.

The core Baptist notions of "priesthood of the believer" and the individual's ability to interpret scripture are populist at their core. This is not pure liberalism, attuned only to the rights of each individual, but an affirmation of the common sense of the common man. The democracy inherent in Southern Baptist polity—especially in its earlier, more consensual form—celebrated the belief that I am as good as you are. The messenger system of voting is itself built on the notion that each believer should come to the convention to speak as an individual Baptist and not as a representative of others.

Another parallel between southern populism, southern democracy, and SBC polity suggests itself. Until recently, the South was dominated by the Democratic political party. The development of a genuine Republican party presence came at roughly the same time as the advent of competing-interest politics in the SBC. In both the SBC and the broader south, opposing the establishment and the bureaucracy of "good old boys" on principle became morally and politically legitimate. Moreover, the organized opposition became respectable.

Although other denominations might be called "populist," the SBC is the largest denomination most clearly associated with a region that could be so designated. But populism is not the only unique Southern Baptist feature contributing to the controversy.

Southern Baptists are fiercely congregationalist, even though they also exhibit a high degree of denominational loyalty.[1] During even the darkest moments of the crisis, there was never a suggestion that individual churches should not be able to act and to think as they saw fit, calling whomever they wanted as leaders. To be sure, a very few churches were disfellowshiped by local associations—most notably for calling women as pastors—but the national body never directly sought to interfere or intervene in local congregational life. For the most part, they would have had no legal or economic means by which to do so. Southern Baptist congregations own their own buildings and manage their own budgets.

It is difficult to imagine a rebellion just like the SBC's in a denomination with a more episcopal form. In the SBC, local pastors did not have to answer to bishops or district supervisors. Individual congregations could align themselves with any political faction they chose (or with none at all). Each was a potential community for grassroots organizing. Given that, it was much simpler for the SBC members to "choose sides" than it would be for the members of many other denominations. There is simply no effective institutional means for coercing group cohesion.

Another distinctively Southern Baptist feature is its conservative theology. As discussed earlier, the doctrine of biblical inerrancy is widely accepted by Southern Baptists. This is not a group in which a small number of disgruntled conservatives got together to kick the shins of the liberal bu-

1. For more details, see my "Judicious Concentration: Decision Making in the SBC," in Ammerman, ed., *Southern Baptists Observed.*

reaucracy. Although the number who were disgruntled enough to take decisive action may have been fairly small, they were able to appeal to a large majority who shared their conservative social and biblical views.

Other denominations might experience a conservative revolt now and again—indeed, almost all of them do. However, the Southern Baptist case is interesting precisely because the conservatives were able to organize a majority bloc to challenge leaders whom they considered to be too liberal or progressive.

Finally, the Southern Baptist case may be unique because of the socioeconomic class of its members. In a wealthier denomination whose members are heavily invested in the stability of the social status quo, institutional revolution would seem unthinkable. In a much poorer denomination whose members are accustomed to accepting all sorts of authority without recourse, it would have been difficult to establish a lasting movement. But in a middle-to-lower-middle-class denomination located in a region that has experienced recent, massive economic growth, revolutionary change is a live option.

Undoubtedly, many Southern Baptists were attached to the social status quo. Others, perhaps many others, were all too prepared to follow orders. But a large number of Southern Baptists—especially the leaders in growing urban areas frequently styled "the new South"—were both confident of their stature in a changing world and prepared to face the challenges of pluralism and relativism. If fundamentalism is primarily a response to certain conditions of modernity,[2] then we should have expected the impetus for the Southern Baptist revolution to have come from precisely these quarters. Conservative pastors of large, urban, middle-class, independent, conservative Southern Baptist churches were able to form the coalition of rural and urban inerrantists necessary to change the bureaucratic establishment.

The Southern Baptist Convention and the Denominational Type

If the controversy in the SBC is an isolated case, then it is because the various elements mentioned above combine in a unique way in this group. Any single characteristic here attributed to Southern Baptists could, of

2. For more on fundamentalism as distinctively modern, see Ammerman, *Bible Believers*; Hunter, *American Evangelicalism*; and Marsden, *Fundamentalism and American Culture*.

course, be attributed to other groups as well: large, populist, southern, congregational, middle-to-lower-middle-class, theologically conservative, and so on. Any one (or all) of these may be necessary, but never sufficient, causes.

These various characteristics, whether broadly social or specifically religious, should not be viewed in isolation from their *organizational* context. That is, such concepts as socioeconomic class and populism may mean different things in different social settings. To understand Southern Baptists fully, one must understand what such concepts mean in the context of the *denomination* as a type of religious organization.

Typologies of religious organizations have fallen into disfavor in recent years, and not without good reason. What started out for Troeltsch as a sociological mission with a distinctively theological purpose later became a sometimes trivial exercise in academic minutiae. Troeltsch intended his ideal-types of church, sect, and mystic to signify the social forms the truths of Christianity had historically taken and to point toward the possible forms those truths might take in the future.

Historically, *churches* were coextensive with their host culture. They might be part of the state itself. They were bureaucratic and hierarchical, emphasizing the institutional power in the office of clergy and in the sacraments. *Sects* existed as opposition to churches. They emphasized either a charismatic leader or a democratic priesthood of all believers. They promoted an ethic rather than a liturgy. They were hostile toward, or at least indifferent to, the rest of culture. *Mystics*, as the name implies, treated religion in the most individualist, personal way, seeking a personal path toward salvation.

Troeltsch's point was that the modern condition made it impossible for a true church—he cites Medieval Catholicism and Reformation Protestantism as examples—to recapture the social center. Sects, on the other hand, were too particular to appeal to the masses. Mysticism lacked sufficient emphasis on "agape"—or any other essentially "social" message—to win the field. Some new form, some "thought not yet thought," would have to emerge. Troeltsch accepted as an article of faith the idea that the truths of Christianity *would* be expressed, somehow, in a manner appropriate to their social setting.[3]

---

3. Troeltsch was a historian, not a fortune teller. He referred to the possibilities of the future only as "new ideas not yet thought." His goal was not to set limits on the future, but to put it in the context of the past by pointing out not only what had worked but also what had not worked and, even more important, what was not working at the time he wrote. See Troeltsch, *Social Teaching*, esp. pp. 993–1013.

Later typological theory cut the organizational distinctions ever and ever more finely. Niebuhr and Martin used Troeltsch's categories to discuss the emergent denomination type.[4] It is, in fact, reasonable to assume that the denomination might be just the "type" Troeltsch anticipated. Wilson, Johnson, and others looked in more detail at sects and then at cults.[5]

Typological theory did not lose its attractiveness because these theorists or their descendants were wrong. Much of their work still guides the sociology of religion. Typologies lost their luster for two related reasons. First, the western culture of individualism and psychotherapy made membership in religious groups an ever-less-significant predictor of social behavior. Membership in religious groups was seen as "caused" by other social factors, such as ethnic identity, socioeconomic class, and educational level; membership in those groups was considered less likely to "cause" other behaviors. Second, the typological theories got ever further from Troeltsch's conviction that some eternal truth was always seeking an appropriate social form. Widespread acceptance of individualism, relativism, and pluralism made the typological exercise ever more sociological and less theological.

If it is therefore somewhat risky to invoke the concept of a denominational type, it is even riskier not to do so. Our common sense is that the North American religious landscape is dominated by precisely the types of broadly based organizations we call denominations. Although sociology may frequently unmask our common sense as prejudice or superstition, it is wise not to abandon simpler, clearer notions for more complex, obscure ones until facts demand that we do so.

The clearest statement of the denominational type came from David Martin in 1962.[6] Martin noted that any British or North American religious organization one might name could probably be said to have both church-like and sect-like characteristics. Denominations were, almost by definition, a mixture of those two types in a society that had no true "church" that was coextensive with the rest of society.[7] But, he insisted, simply to call the denomination a hybrid was to miss its most important feature: it is precisely

4. Niebuhr, *The Social Sources of Denominationalism*; Martin, "The Denomination."

5. Wilson, "An Analysis of Sect Development"; Benton Johnson, "On Church and Sect," *American Sociological Review* 28 (August 1963), 530–49.

6. Martin, "The Denomination."

7. Troeltsch's church type referred to something more like a "state" or "national" church that was part and parcel of the rest of culture. In such organizations, salvation rested in the organization itself and was administered objectively through the sacraments. Churches were by definition hierarchical, insisting on office and doctrine rather than the virtuosity of particular individuals.

the institutional logic behind mixing qualities once thought of as church-like or sect-like that made denominations a unique type all to themselves.

That institutional logic was individualistic, utilitarian, and pragmatic. Denominations flourished because they did not insist on their version of the truth as the only path to salvation. They appealed to the masses, as churches do, because they have an organized liturgy and catechesis. But they are sufficiently local and particular—like sects—that they can also emphasize an ethic or a "way of life."

The denominational type of organization has succeeded because it is so adaptable. Like a church, it provides an *organizational base* for religious practice and belief. It can have a formal hierarchy of authority. But unlike the church, it does not insist that grace or truth resides in the organization itself. Denominations can also be very democratic. Indeed, they are always more democratic, more governed from below, than any organization that insists that the grace is in the form of the group rather than in the individual. Because denominations turn to the individual, each organization, each denomination, is malleable. It can shape itself to meet the present social circumstances.

Such malleability is not universally regarded as a strength. To some, this sort of pragmatism seems unprincipled. But in a western world frequently thought of as "secularized," where religious institutions have ceded the power to shape and control much of society, the numbers of North Americans who still claim to believe in God and who attend worship regularly are very high by western standards. What looks like the failure of organized religion to some[8]—the church splitting into many smaller organizations—looks to others like brilliant marketing strategy.[9] In societies characterized by a high degree of denominationalism, there is something for everyone. If the congregation or group one is now in does not meet one's social, ideological, and therapeutic needs, there are many more to choose from.

Thus denominations cater to individuals. They need not be excessively rigorous, like sects, but neither do they emphasize the organization as the vehicle of grace at the individual's expense. They do what they need to do to survive; they spread their message in the form best suited to its audience.

Seen in this light, denominations meet precisely the requirements Troeltsch set for those "thoughts not yet thought." They are the religious

8. This is, after all, precisely the claim of Niebuhr in his *Social Sources of Denominationalism.*

9. Berger (*The Sacred Canopy*) notes the propensity of modern religious organizations to market themselves. This is necessary because there is no shared "plausibility" structure, no taken-for-grantedness, on which any one organization can hope to draw.

organizational form exactly suited to individualistic, democratic, pluralistic, consumerist societies. Martin wanted to claim "no more than a connection" between denominations and the cultures in which they flourish, but it seems possible now to say more. Denominations embody many of the liberal notions that distinguish Britain and North America.

What does this sociological description of the denominational type have to do with Southern Baptists? Some would argue that it has nothing to do with it, that Southern Baptists are mostly sect-like with an emphasis on a conservative ethic of biblical legalism and hyperindividualism.[10] But such arguments are wrongheaded. Southern Baptists embody the denominational type and share the liberal ideas common to that type and to the rest of American culture, in the strongest possible way.

By its sheer size, the SBC renders any attempt to call it something other than a denomination meaningless. This is a group that appeals to masses of culture. In fact, in some southern areas the SBC probably functions more like a church—inasmuch as it is broadly coextensive with the rest of local culture—than most other groups in the United States. Of course, outside of the South the SBC can look very sectarian.

Quibbling about typological classification is a pedantic waste of time. The point is not that the Southern Baptist Convention "should" be called a denomination. The point is that it shares with other groups we call "denominations" in everyday discourse many of the characteristics that make the denominational type a meaningful designation.

The SBC, as any other denomination group, combines features that might seem church-like with those that seem sect-like. Some congregations have charismatic leaders or strict democracy, others emphasize the bureaucratic office of leadership (as does the larger group). At some points the SBC seems outside of mainstream culture—for instance, its staunch opposition to abortion rights seems at least illiberal. At other points, the SBC is quite mainstream. There are very good reasons to believe that the majority of Southern Baptists have voted for the winning presidential candidate in every election at least since 1972.[11] Too often theorists who would place Southern Baptists

10. Even Meredith McGuire, in her excellent and even-handed textbook (*Religion: The Social Context*, 3rd ed. [New York: Wadsworth Publishing, 1992]), does not list Southern Baptists among the denominations (p. 140).

11. Center for Religious Research data suggest that Southern Baptists have gradually moved from the conservative wing of the Democratic party to the Republican party. Although there is no irrefutable evidence on this score, it is probable that Southern Baptists supported Nixon over McGovern. They probably did support the more liberal Carter over Ford, because Carter was both southern and Southern Baptist and Ford was not particularly conservative. Southern Baptist voting in the Reagan-Carter election would be very difficult to determine, but I have

outside of the mainstream because of their staunch conservatism fail to see just how politically *and* biblically conservative a large part of American culture is.

What is at stake here is not that this argument convinces anyone to label the SBC in this or that way. What is at stake is the claim that the SBC shares with other denominations a kind of *procedural, organizational* commitment to individualism and pragmatism. The details may be different: Episcopalians are more liturgical and hierarchical; Presbyterians are better educated; Lutherans have more formal ethnic ties, and so on. But differences in class, status, region, or even ecclesiology cannot obscure the basic similarities: denominations look to the individual, and in so doing replicate the pragmatic, liberal, American culture in which they reside. Recognizing that fact does not require one to ignore all the unique features of Southern Baptist life and to conclude that everyone else should expect the same set of circumstances and experiences. The unique features are important. But the common features also deserve our theoretical and, for better or worse, practical attention.

General and Specific Lessons

Only Southern Baptists can decide for themselves whether the turmoil of the 1980s was worth the price. That price includes a large chunk of the denomination—probably ultimately something like 10 percent—that no longer cooperates with national programs in any significant way. It also includes more than a little ill-will between individuals in the SBC and between the SBC and many outside observers, at least in the short run. What was gained is equally clear: all of the denomination's programs and schools are now controlled by self-professed inerrantists. Those who wanted to bring the Convention "back" to its roots of biblical inerrancy have succeeded, at least in organizational terms.

Some fundamentalist Southern Baptists have argued that, in the long run, the price has not been that high. Those who have left had no business in the SBC in the first place. Moreover, they say, the personal rancor was overstated by the losing moderates and by the liberal press. W. A. Criswell,

---

heard more than one Southern Baptist say that he regretted voting for Carter the first time. There is little doubt that Southern Baptists voted for Reagan over Dukakis and for Bush over Mondale.

who was remarkably restrained at the 1991 Atlanta meeting given his side's sweeping victory, called the moderates who had left or who were still complaining "flies on an elephant's behind."

Others in the conservative-but-more-moderate middle doubtless regret the loss of fellowship even if they consider it a necessary and inevitable cost. They would have liked, in good American fashion, more of a compromise, less of a winner-take-all battle. It is unclear whether a more moderate strategy would have worked, but now that the crisis is over it is possible to review and analyze the features that led to conflict rather than compromise.

It seems clear enough that the former moderate establishment both underestimated and undervalued fundamentalist ideology. Fundamentalist leaders claim they used to be excluded; the old moderates dispute that claim. Without rehashing or extending an already extensive historical argument, one can say that there are good reasons to believe that the old bureaucracy intended to dismiss fundamentalism when it believed it could do so. The old guard was never truly "liberal" by any national standard, despite fundamentalists' claims. Just the same, the leadership was much friendlier to the academic notions of historical criticism and evolution than were most of their constituents.

The populist assumptions of cooperation and consensus—and their organizational embodiment in the sending of messengers—were never reevaluated in the light of changing demographic patterns in membership. Whichever side was winning cited the old assumptions as a weapon against their challengers. Moderates said to the angry fundamentalists, "The bureaucracy was put here by the messengers," knowing full well that the messengers usually comprised a very small percentage of the group—and the more educated, better-off, more liberal wing at that. Fundamentalists, after they had exploited the loose democratic mechanisms in the messenger system, said to the moderates, "We won fair and square." Given the existing rules, it is clear that they did.

When the fundamentalist challenges grew in the 1970s, the moderates had the opportunity to make the cooperative system of government more representative. They could also have built in safeguards—some sorts of membership rights or proportional representation—for the minority opposition. Their failure to do either of these things haunted them as they became the minority. They had little recourse; they could not even point to the goodwill they had shown when they were on top because, for the most part, they gave no better than they were now getting.

Why were safeguards such as guarantees of member's rights or proportionality ignored? One reason is that whoever was winning benefited from the old rules that ill-fit the new, pluralistic denomination. But a deeper ideological reason cited earlier still lurks beneath that self-interest: Southern Baptists never wanted to admit that the group had, in fact, become polarized. Their insistence on a commonsense reading of the Bible and on each individual's path to God led them away from admitting the possibility that there could be honest differences about the most fundamental points. Some truths were still absolute, and those who did not agree were just wrong, even if the organization's means for settling those disputes required democratic procedures better suited to relativism than to absolutism.

For many of these same reasons, victorious fundamentalists could not even reach out to the dispossesed (and rapidly leaving) moderates in any meaningful way. They were willing to make some organizational concessions—to invest authority in Richard Jackson even if some of them considered him a traitor, or to leave certain moderate functionaries in place—but they were unwilling and unable to make any concessions on theology or ideology.

Some of the animosity and the worst of the bloodletting might then have been avoided had certain organizational procedures been changed. However, neither side was willing to make those changes, and there is no reason to believe that the current victors would make them if they had it all to do over again. In this regard, the unique Southern Baptist emphasis on individualism and biblical conservatism makes it difficult to say that there is any specific organizational lesson here for Baptists to learn. In the future, challenges may well be handled in much the same way, despite the inevitable pain and division. The doctrine of inerrancy, enforced politically, requires no less. Whether this process whittles the SBC ever thinner depends on the continued viability of biblical inerrancy as a twentieth-century ideology. If fundamentalism recedes, the SBC is likely to recede with it. If fundamentalism flourishes, so will the Convention.

The organizational lessons might then best be directed toward others. The first and most obvious lesson is that serious theological dissent is ignored at the peril of the larger group. Paul Harrison warned American Baptists that if they continued to ignore the fundamentalists in their ranks they would eventually have to pay a high price. The old hierarchy in the SBC found out just how high that price could be.

No denomination among the contemporary "mainline" is immune to the same sort of dissent. Many United Methodists believe that their denomination's bureaucracy is too liberal. Conservatives in the United Methodist Church are dismayed by policies in the denomination's seminaries that pro-

scribe the use of masculine pronouns for God or support a homosexual life-
style. These Methodist conservatives have already called on their seminaries
to "teach theology that is consistent with the theological statement in our
Book of Discipline."[12] It does not take much imagination to see seeds of controversy very much like those present twenty years ago in the SBC when
United Methodist conservatives call for "corrective therapy for our seminaries."

Presbyterians saw in the summer of 1991 that the same progressive policies
that appeal to the denominational elite—in this case, a document on sexuality with some nontraditional recommendations concerning homosexuality
and sex outside of marriage—are a red flag waved at moral conservatives in
the group. The document on sexuality was a proposal researched by a special
committee. It recommended consideration of homosexual unions, set moral
conditions for sex outside of marriage, and explored other nontraditional
views of sexuality. The document was not technically defeated because it
was not really ever proposed as a change of doctrine or confession. The
national body simply decided not to accept the recommendations of the
study committee at this time. Nonetheless, the issue was widely regarded as
a rejection of a liberal, "establishment" policy by a more conservative laity.

Numbers of Episcopalians are challenging their progressive establishment
in a sort of "reform" movement. In a special meeting in 1992, Episcopal
bishops vowed to emphasize prayer and deemphasize politics in their future
meetings. This meeting was called to address concerns that feuding factions
in the 1991 General Assembly threatened the health of the organization.
This feud also centered on the practice of "extramarital sex," including homosexual relations, by Episcopal clergy. Some dissident reformers have already established their own diocese, and some churches have left the denomination.[13]

In none of these cases is it likely that a conservative majority will over-
throw the established hierarchy as it did in the SBC. Very possibly none of
these groups have a conservative majority. The fact that each of these controversies hinges on traditional sexual morality points out their difference
from the Southern Baptists. It is difficult to imagine any Southern Baptist
(except for a minute fringe element) advocating serious changes in traditional moral attitudes toward homosexuality or extramarital relations.

12. Position paper from the Legislative Strategy Team of Good News.
13. Julia Din, "Episcopal Bishops Agree to Less Debate, More Prayer in Future," Atlanta
Journal and Constitution, March 21, 1992.

In every single one of these cases, however, the larger organization would do well to consider the insitutionalization of minority "rights" such as channels for leadership, expression of theological opinions, and educational opportunities. Americans—nearly all of whom are steeped in individualism and democracy—do not blush at the prospect of having to squeeze their organizations to make them fit their ideas and experiences. The conservatives who found a voice in the late 1970s and early 1980s are not likely soon to be silent.[14]

Not only have those conservatives found a voice, but they have found also that there is power in *political-style organizing*. Not every denomination is as vulnerable to organized political attack as the SBC, but no denomination is immune to a well-organized, concerted effort to change its policies. The groundswell of conservative disapproval among Presbyterians opposed to the documents on sexuality only suggests the potential for political organizing. Conservatives apparently "won" and did not need to press the matter further. If the issue does not die down, however, and if future reports continue to suggest more tolerant, nontraditional views of sexuality, a better-organized opposition is likely to appear.

Political entities like the Moral Majority or Operation Rescue or even Pat Robertson's presidential campaign may or may not represent a genuine majority opinion. Their limited successes suggest that they do not. But the fact that they exist as parachurch, religiopolitical organizations means that every denomination is always open to organized, concerted political pressure. There is always already an organized power-base on which dissatisfied conservatives can draw. Fundamentalists in the SBC used the existing nonofficial organizations—such as Mid-American seminary or the fundamentalist presses—as a platform from which to launch their successful "official" attack.

The other lesson that must not be overlooked is the susceptibility of the denominational type of organization to political-style change. Even the most episcopal of the denominations differ from a true church type of organization insofar as they admit that grace is not inherent in the organization itself. That is, denominations rarely style themselves as the unique repository of truth and salvation, accessible only through *their* sacraments administered by *their* leaders. Precisely this sort of pluralism led Martin to call denominations

14. Many claims about the connection between fundamentalists and the success of political conservatives are surely overblown. Pat Robertson's miserably failed presidential campaign put the lie to the notion that fundamentalists elected President Reagan. However, there does seem to be a connection between recent grassroots organizing by both religious and political conservatives. If nothing else, the "silent majority" has found its voice in both.

"pragmatic." The organization itself is not the "body of Christ," but simply a group—called or gathered—in which that body resides.

Given that pragmatism, there is nothing inherently sacred about the organization or its leaders. In the most blunt summary of the matter, if grace is ultimately in the individuals or at least in the persons (perhaps communally) rather than in the organization, then the organization gets its authority from those people. Denominations, no matter how hierarchical, get their authority from the "bottom up." Any such organization—be it a local community or a nation or a denomination—carries within itself the seeds of its own change or even destruction. Every such organization is ultimately susceptible to democratic or popular pressure, even if the group is not especially populist or democratic. In a liberal nation like the United States, where nearly everyone thinks of himself or herself as a freely choosing individual, that pressure to "democratize" or "popularize" is all the greater.[15]

Denominations therefore "market" themselves to key constituencies much as political parties or candidates do. That process makes perfect sense in our society: individuals or small groups based on ethnic or familial ties align themselves around locale or particular issues and practices. These small alliances link up with other similar ones in ever larger clusters, sometimes along ethnic or cultural lines, sometimes along political lines, and sometimes around economic interest. These larger groups then form fluid clusters at the level of state or national organizations. The clusters are "fluid" precisely because they shift from candidate to candidate, party to party, business to business.

In the context of increasing pluralism, denominations also take on this fluid character. They are, finally, mutable clusters of individuals or small groups organized around ethnic ties or region or specific ideas. The more varied and pluralistic these bigger clusters become, the more we should expect smaller groups within them to press for changes—at least changes of emphasis—in specific ideas or programs. In the American context of individualism, democracy, and the power of popular opinion, it should not be surprising that such pressure is applied through political means. Political pressure requires a renewed emphasis on the organizational *procedures* by which change can be effected.

---

15. Robert Bellah et al.'s recent books, *Habits of the Heart* (1985) and *The Good Society* (New York: Publishing, 1991), make a strong case for the dominance of this individualism. Even in the very "church-like" Roman Catholic church, Americans expect a high degree of autonomy and democratic or popular input. See Dennis McCann, *New Experiment in Democracy: The Challenge for American Catholicism* (New York: Sheed & Ward, 1987).

Not every denomination will have the same sort of loose procedures found in the SBC. In fact, probably no other large group has such an ill-defined yet somewhat representative system for choosing leaders and policies. But every denomination will do well to look at its *procedures* and to evaluate the effectiveness of those procedures at allowing dissent and institutionalizing mechanisms for change.

One possible objection to such a suggestion is that it calls on denominations to abandon their theological principles in favor of organizational pragmatism. After all, should not the procedures be based on truth or on scripture rather than on some utilitarian notion of "workability." The only response to that objection is that the denominations themselves have institutionalized pluralism, individualism, and dissent. In short, *they are pragmatic already*, governed by a rationalized ethos forged in the crucible of a highly rationalized society. No sectarian desire for purity or a return to "the true church" will put this genie back in the bottle, because even theological debate about what is "pure" or "true" is subject to these individualistic and democratic sorts of popular pressure. If the debate focuses on the wishes of individuals, and if the authority to make changes rests with them, the organization cannot then pretend that it somehow represents a higher or greater reality.

Given that, denominations can either attempt to elucidate and protect their ideological and social boundaries, letting both the chips and their members fall where they may, or they can institutionalize within their organizations the procedures necessary to deal with increasing pluralism. They can circle the wagons, insisting on specific requirements for membership, or they can emphasize toleration and diversity. Now is the time to choose, because ultimately each denomination will do one or the other.

Conclusion

There is nothing novel about the suggestion that American religion is "individualistic" or "popular" or even "political." In 1835 de Tocqueville called religion in the New World "a form of Christianity which I cannot better describe than by styling it a democratic and republican religion." He went on to say:

> In the United States even the religion of most of the citizens is republican, since it submits the truths of the other world to private judgment, as in politics the care of their temporal interests is abandoned to the good sense of the people. Thus every man is allowed freely to take that road which he thinks will lead him to heaven, just as the law permits every citizen to have the right of choosing his own government.[1]

But recognition of these unique features of American religion is not enough. It is one thing to say that the religious enterprise contributes to the common good because people find in religion many of the values necessary to support a free and liberal state. It is quite another thing to ask what effect the liberal values embodied in that state have on the integrity of the religious organizations. De Tocqueville demonstrated the benefits of religion for, and the effects of religion on, the republic. It is just as important to recognize the effect that the republic, now an enormous bureaucratic forum for a multitude of competing interests, has on religion.

Put another way, there is more than one way to ask questions about "church and state." Much attention has been paid to issues concerning the

---

1. Alexis de Tocqueville, *Democracy in America*, trans. George Lawrence, ed. J. P. Mayer (1835; reprint, Garden City, N.Y.: Doubleday, 1969), p. 288.

interference of the state in religious matters *and* to tendencies of the state to favor or to promote any particular religion. Much less has been said about the far-reaching effects that the liberal, democratic *model* of government has had on other organizations.

Descriptions of the controversy in the SBC can follow many lines: it is a theological dispute, a division between socioeconomic classes, a clash of different cultures, and a reaction to "modern" ideas about change and progress. However the controversy is described, the crux of the issue is *pluralism.* How has the Convention dealt with a plurality of theological beliefs, social classes, or cultural assumptions?

It would be both socially convenient and theologically pure if problems caused by pluralism and difference were always settled either by compromise or by one side accepting the other's good arguments. Although compromise is itself an essential American prerogative, religious disputes are seldom settled in this manner. The stakes—eternal salvation and God's continued blessings—are too high to allow for some mutually profitable arrangement. There is just no room to "give." Besides, in American society it is far too easy to start a new group that emphasizes whatever difference originally led to the problem.

In this American milieu of individualism, pluralism, and freedom to associate, there are no formal constraints on membership in religious organizations. That is not to say that there are not many informal ones; ethnic ties, socioeconomic class, educational levels, and many other factors play a role in religious-group identity. But there is no formal or official coercion to join or to avoid any group. There is no Church of America and, at least outside of Utah, no broad presumption of membership in any particular organization.[2]

In this fluid, malleable context, membership and standing are matters handled internally by the organizations themselves. It should be no surprise, then, that the organization's *procedures* come to the fore when confronted by the pressures of increasing pluralism. As groups expand, as the boundaries and the identities of their constituencies are challenged, they have no choice but to rely on the *polity* already in place to deal with questions about diversity in membership, in beliefs, and in practices.

On at least one level, then, understanding a group's polity is the key to

---

2. I have often remarked to my students in sociology of religion courses that a trip to Salt Lake City caused me to tone down any definitive statements that no religious organization in America functions as a church as Troeltsch conceived it.

understanding its prospects for dealing with the problems pluralism can cause. Each unique group requires specific analysis; the evidence must be evaluated on a case-by-case basis.

The Southern Baptist Convention is an especially interesting case for several reasons. It is the largest Protestant denomination in North America. It has had decidedly American, liberal (in the classical sense) ideas, such as individualism and pragmatism and democracy, built into its polity from the beginning, even though its culture is very conservative. Its current controversy breaks down along conservative and liberal (in the contemporary sense) lines that define many other groups on both the theological and political spectrum.[3]

Because each denomination has its own unique characteristics, the case-study format makes the most sense. Subtle differences between groups—in class divisions, cultural incompatibility, theology, or even the polity's nuts-and-bolts—could lead to very different analyses of their situations. But that is not to say that there are no common elements or that more general observations are impossible. A large theoretical framework already exists to guide specific case studies. Each of these studies can measure its data against that framework and then, in turn, measure the theories against the new data. When enough data is available, it may even be possible to construct general theories capable of marshaling it.

The case of the Southern Baptists suggests several intriguing possiblities. One possibility is that the political model of "competing interests" has become the dominant mode of conflict resolution in America. Even in this theologically conservative group, doctrinal differences were settled by democratic procedure. Even in this relatively homogeneous organization (as compared with American society as a whole), differences were settled by ballot and eventually led to unofficial political limits on membership and participation. Even in this culturally conservative milieu, the classically liberal notion of individual choice paced the changes.

All of these elements point out that despite conservative tendencies linked to ideology, region, or culture, the pragmatic nature of the organization inclined it toward models of decision-making that are liberal, popular,

---

3. The conservative-liberal split in American politics defies any simple description, but some basic division along these lines is so simple as to be commonsensical. For an excellent description of that split in American religion, see Wuthnow's *Restructuring of American Religion*. Wuthnow goes so far as to argue that the conservative-liberal distinction (including the evangelical-progressive split) is replacing denominational difference as the defining characteristic of American religious life.

and democratic. In a word, *procedure* dominates even here. That procedure, including the images of competing interests and well-defined rules and boundaries it evokes, *is the spirit of politics infused into every corner of American life.* Businesses, schools, and even religious organizations must acknowledge the prominence of procedural norms derived from the state.

This does not mean that every organization must then concede its affairs to political maneuvering. Different organizations, whether economic or religious, have their own internal logic suited to their particular goals and needs. But only by recognizing the power of the "political" within itself can each organization evaluate its practices in order to decide how much "politics" is appropriate. Many elements within the Southern Baptist Convention failed to appreciate just how important this competing interest model was to their situation. Other religious organizations would do well to look to their own polities in this regard.

Another interesting possibility is that this "politicization" will have a moderating effect on organizations in the long run. The lure of competing interest models for decision-making is that they establish right and wrong—a winner and a loser—in a group lacking enough of a consensus to establish such values through fiat or compromise. Put another way, politics settles questions that cannot be settled in any other manner. The losers do not have to be convinced of their error; they only have to be convinced that the procedure was fair and that the majority went against them. In this way, competing interest models work fine even for rigorous fundamentalists, *if they remain the majority and can therefore continue to win.*

The risk of this sort of politics is that it tends to pull all sides toward the middle. Once a group has admitted that right and wrong will be determined by majority rule, it has also admitted that it is open to the ongoing alignment and realignment of parties and coalitions within it. Anyone observing an arena of "competing interests" soon learns that there are *many* interests competing. Insofar as the conflict in the SBC concerned only two interests—biblical inerrantists and progressives—the political procedures settled the issue uneqivocally. But there are many other interests—different views of missions, of pastoral authority, of secular politics—that are not nearly so settled. The SBC is subject to the pushes and pulls of different coalitions as the parties formed around the biblical dispute dissolve and new coalitions emerge around different kinds of issues.

The point is not that the SBC will have permanent, continuous unrest. It is more stable just now than it has been in more than a decade. But the genie is out of the bottle and cannot be put back in. The new SBC, defined by its boundaries of loose inerrancy, can expect new politics in the future. The state conventions already show that ambiguity. In Georgia, in Texas, and elsewhere, the presidency and the bureaucracy shift back and forth between groups previously aligned with both of the two competing parties. One year fundamentalists win, another year moderates win. The new "taken-for-grantedness" in the national organization has not trickled down to all of the states and may never do so.

This kind of politics has the moderating effect of drawing the debate toward the center. As in American national politics, candidates build coalitions from a variety of disparate groups with different, if not indeed oppositional, interests. Those who are too radical or reactionary may draw strong support from their own quarter, but they seldom make attractive national candidates. Single issues may serve as lightning rods now and again, but they cannot do that forever.

Will the moderating tendencies of liberal politics—coalition-building and respect for individual difference—eventually draw the SBC back toward its new, admittedly more conservative center? It is too early to tell, but some signs suggest that they yet may. Nothing in the tone or the actions of the 1991 meeting portends continued hostility. Events in the state conventions continue to reflect balance and at least a little more calm than they had ten years ago. How will that moderation set with the most ardent fundamentalists? There is no way to say for certain, but it is likely that the most committed will find any concessions intolerable and could either leave or curtail their cooperation with the Convention.

Any discussion concerning the future of politics in the SBC or other religious organizations is necessarily tenuous. At best, the analytical framework informing this case study exists as an open invitation to others concerned about the role of "politics" in the polity of other religious organizations.

Any lessons to be learned must be more general than specific, because the question is not, finally, "How is any other group like or unlike the SBC?" but "What is the relationship of political procedure to the denominational type of religious organization?" If this study has used one case to suggest some answers to that question, then it has fit one brick into a structure that is changing even as it is built.

Bibliography

Ahlstrom, Sydney. *A Religious History of the American People*. New Haven: Yale University Press, 1972.

Ammerman, Nancy. "After the Battles: Emerging Organizational Forms for Baptists." In *Southern Baptists Observed*, ed. Nancy Ammerman. Knoxville: University of Tennessee Press, 1993.

———. *Baptist Battles: Social Change and Religious Conflict in the Southern Baptist Convention*. New Brunswick, N.J.: Rutgers University Press, 1990.

———. *The Bible Believers*. New Brunswick, N.J.: Rutgers University Press, 1987.

———. "The New South and the New Baptists." *Christian Century*, May 14, 1986.

———. "North American Protestant Fundamentalism." In *Fundamentalisms Observed*, ed. Martin E. Marty and R. Scott Appleby. Chicago: University of Chicago Press, 1990.

Ammerman, Nancy, ed. *Southern Baptists Observed: Multiple Perspectives on a Changing Denomination*. Knoxville: University of Tennessee Press, 1993.

Anderson, Robert. *Vision of the Disinherited*. New York: Oxford Press, 1979.

Baker, Robert. *A Baptist Source Book*. Nashville, Tenn.: Broadman Press, 1966.

———. *The Southern Baptist Convention and Its People, 1607–1972*. Nashville, Tenn.: Broadman Press, 1974.

Barnes, William. *The Southern Baptist Convention, 1845–1953*. Nashville, Tenn.: Broadman Press, 1954.

Barnhart, Joseph. *The Southern Baptist Holy War*. Austin: Texas Monthly Press, 1986.

Bellah, Robert. *Beyond Belief: Essays on Religion in a Post-Traditional World*. New York: Harper & Row, 1970.

Bellah, Robert, et al. *Habits of the Heart: Individualism and Commitment in American Life*. Berkeley and Los Angeles: University of California Press, 1985.

———. *The Good Society*. New York: Knopf, 1991.

Berger, Peter. *The Noise of Solemn Assemblies: Christian Commitment and the Religious Establishment in America*. Garden City, N.Y.: Doubleday, 1961.

———. *The Sacred Canopy*. Garden City, N.Y.: Doubleday, 1961.

Berger, Peter, and Thomas Luckmann. *The Social Construction of Reality*. Garden City, N.Y.: Doubleday, 1966.

Bromley, David, and Anson Shupe. *The New Christian Politics*. Macon, Ga.: Mercer University Press, 1984.

De Camp, L. Sprague. *The Great Monkey Trial*. Garden City, N.Y.: Doubleday, 1968.

Draper, James. *Authority: The Critical Issue for Southern Baptists*. Old Tappan, N.J.: Fleming Revell, 1984.

Durkheim, Emile. *The Elementary Forms of the Religious Life: A Study in Religious Sociology.* Translated by Joseph Ward Swain. New York: Macmillan, 1915.

Egerton, John. *The Americanization of Dixie, the Southernization of America.* New York: Harper & Row, 1974.

Eighmy, John. *Churches in Cultural Captivity.* Knoxville: University of Tennessee Press, 1972.

Elliott, Ralph. *The Message of Genesis.* Nashville, Tenn.: Broadman Press, 1961.

Farnsley, Arthur. "Judicious Concentration: Decision-Making in the Southern Baptist Convention." In *Southern Baptists Observed,* ed. Nancy Ammerman. Knoxville: University of Tennessee Press, 1993.

———. "The Relationship of Belief to Institutional Location in Moral Decision-Making: The Case of the SBC." Paper presented to the Association for the Sociology of Religion, Atlanta, Georgia, August 1988.

Furniss, Norman. *The Fundamentalist Controversy, 1918–1931.* Hamden, Conn.: Archon Books, 1963.

Gatewood, Willard. *Controversy in the 1920s: Fundamentalism, Modernism, and Evolution.* Nashville, Tenn.: Vanderbilt University Press, 1969.

Geertz, Clifford. *The Interpretation of Cultures.* New York: Basic Books, 1973.

Ginger, Ray. *Six Days or Forever: Tennessee Versus John Thomas Scopes.* Boston: Beacon Press, 1958.

Goffman, Erving. *The Presentation of Self in Everyday Life.* 1956. Reprint. Garden City, N.Y.: Doubleday, 1959.

Greenspahn, Frederick, and Martin E. Marty, eds. *Pushing the Faith: Proselytism and Civility in a Pluralistic World.* New York: Crossroads Press, 1988.

Hadden, Jeffery. "Religious Broadcasting and the New Christian Right." Presidential address to the Society for the Scientific Study of Religion. Reprinted in *Journal for the Scientific Study of Religion* 26 (March 1987).

Hadden, Jeffrey, and Anson Shupe. *Televangelism.* New York: Huff, 1988.

———. "Is Pat Robertson About to Embarrass God?" Paper delivered to the Society for the Scientific Study of Religion, Louisville, Kentucky, October 1987.

Harrison, Paul. *Authority and Power in the Free Church Tradition: A Social Case Study of the American Baptist Convention.* Princeton: Princeton University Press, 1959.

Hefley, James. *The Truth in Crisis: The Controversy in the Southern Baptist Convention.* Vols. 1, 2, 3, 4. Dallas: Criterion Publications, 1986–89.

Heinz, Donald. "The Struggle to Define America." In *The New Christian Right,* ed. Robert Liebman and Robert Wuthnow. New York: Aldine, 1983.

Hill, Samuel, et al. *Religion and the Solid South.* New York: Abingdon Press, 1972.

Hinson, Glenn. "Southern Baptist Fundamentalists Stirring up a Storm." *Christian Century,* July 18–25, 1979, pp. 725–27.

Hobbs, Herschel. *What Baptists Believe.* Nashville, Tenn.: Broadman Press, 1964.

Hunter, James. *American Evangelicalism.* New Brunswick, N.J.: Rutgers University Press, 1983.

Johnson, Benton. "On Church and Sect." *American Sociological Review* 28 (August 1963), 539–49.

Johnson, Stephen, Joseph Tamney, and Ronald Burton. "Vote for a Christian Right Candidate." Paper delivered to the Society for the Sociological Study of Religion, Louisville, Kentucky, October 1987.

Jorstad, Erling. *The New Christian Right, 1981–1988: Prospects for the Post-Reagan Decade.* Lewiston, N.Y.: Mellen Press, 1987.

Kant, Immanuel. *The Critique of Pure Reason; The Critique of Practical Reason and Other*

Ethical Treatises; The Critique of Judgement. Translated by John M. D. Meiklejohn. Chicago: Encyclopaedia Brittanica, 1990.

Kanter, Rosabeth Moss. *Commitment and Community: Communes and Utopias in Sociological Perspective.* Cambridge, Mass.: Harvard Press, 1982.

Lechner, Frank. "Fundamentalism and Sociocultural Revitalization in America: A Sociological Interpretation." *Sociological Analysis* 46, no. 3 (March 1985), 243–60.

———. "Modernity and Its Discontents." In *Neofunctionalism,* ed. Jeffrey Alexander. Beverly Hills, Calif.: Sage Publications, 1985.

Leonard, Bill J. *God's Last and Only Hope: The Fragmentation of the Southern Baptist Convention.* Grand Rapids, Mich.: Eerdmans Publishing Co., 1990.

Liebman, Robert, and Robert Wuthnow, eds. *The New Christian Right.* New York: Aldine, 1983.

Lindsell, Harold. *The Bible in the Balance.* Grand Rapids, Mich.: Zondervan Publishing House, 1979.

Marsden, George. *Fundamentalism and American Culture: The Shaping of 20th Century Evangelicalism.* New York: Oxford University Press, 1980.

Martin, David. "The Denomination." *British Journal of Sociology* 13 (January 1962), 1–13.

———. *The Dilemmas of Contemporary Religion.* New York: St. Martin's Press, 1978.

McCann, Dennis. *New Experiment in Democracy: The Challenge for American Catholicism.* New York: Sheed & Ward, 1987.

McClellan, Albert. *The Executive Committee of the Southern Baptist Convention, 1917–1984.* Nashville, Tenn.: Broadman Press, 1985.

McDaniel, George. *The Churches of the New Testament.* New York: Richard Smith, 1921.

McGuire, Meredith. *Religion: The Social Context.* 3rd ed. New York: Wadsworth, 1992.

Meyer, John, and Brian Rowan. "Institutionalized Organizations: Formal Structure as Myth and Ceremony." *American Journal of Sociology* 83 (September 1977), 340–63.

Meyer, John, and W. Richard Scott. *Organizational Environments: Ritual and Rationality.* Beverly Hills, Calif.: Sage Publications, 1983.

Mills, C. Wright. *White Collar: The American Middle Classes.* New York: Oxford University Press, 1951.

Niebuhr, H. Richard. *The Social Sources of Denominationalism.* New York: Henry Holt & Co., 1929.

Parsons, Talcott. *The Social System.* Glencoe, Ill.: The Free Press, 1951.

———. *Social Systems and the Evolution of Action Theory.* Glencoe, Ill.: The Free Press, 1977.

Primer, Benjamin. *The Bureaucratization of the Church: Protestant Response to Modern, Large-Scale Organization, 1876–1929.* Ph.D. dissertation, Johns Hopkins University, 1977.

Rosenberg, Ellen. *The Southern Baptists: A Subculture in Transition.* Knoxville: University of Tennessee Press, 1989.

Rossiter, Clinton. *The American Presidency.* New York: Harcourt Brace, 1976.

Russell, C. Allyn. *Voices of American Fundamentalists: Seven Biographical Stories.* Philadelphia: Westminster Press, 1976.

Sandeen, Ernest. *The Roots of Fundamentalism: British and American Millenarianism, 1800–1930.* Chicago: University of Chicago Press, 1970.

Scalf, John, Michael Miller, and Charles Thomas. "Goal Specificity, Organizational Structure, and Participant Commitment in Churches." *Sociological Analysis* 34, no. 3 (Fall 1973), 169–84.

Schluchter, Wolfgang. "The Future of Religion." In *Religion and America*, ed. Mary Douglas and Steven Tipton. Boston: Beacon Press, 1982.
———. *The Rise of Western Rationalism*. Berkeley and Los Angeles: University of California Press, 1981.
Scopes, John, and James Presley. *Center of the Storm: Memoirs of John T. Scopes*. New York: Holt, Rinehart & Winston, 1967.
Shibley, Mark. "The Southernization of American Religion: Testing a Hypothesis." *Sociological Analysis* 52, no. 2 (1991), 159–74.
Smith, Adam. *An Inquiry into the Nature and Causes of the Wealth of Nations*. 1776. Reprint. Indianapolis, Ind.: Liberty Press, 1976.
———. *The Theory of Moral Sentiments*. 1759. Reprint. Indianapolis, Ind.: Liberty Press, 1976.
Stempien, Richard, and Sarah Coleman. "Processes of Persuasion." *Review of Religious Research* 27 (December 1985), 169–77.
Sullivan, James. *Baptist Polity as I See It*. Nashville, Tenn.: Broadman Press, 1983.
———. *Southern Baptist Polity at Work in a Church*. Nashville, Tenn.: Broadman Press, 1987.
Tipton, Steven, and Mary Douglas, eds. *Religion and America*. Boston: Beacon Press, 1982.
Tocqueville, Alexis de. *Democracy in America*. 1835. Translated by George Lawrence. Edited by J. P. Mayer. Garden City, N.Y.: Doubleday, 1969.
Tompkins, Jerry. *D-Days at Dayton: Reflections on the Scopes Trial*. Baton Rouge: Louisiana State University Press, 1965.
Torbet, Robert. *A History of the Baptists*. Philadelphia: Judson Press, 1950.
Troeltsch, Ernst. *The Social Teaching of the Christian Churches*. Translated by Olive Wyon. 1911. Reprint. Chicago: University of Chicago Press, 1960.
Turner, Helen. "Myths: Stories of This World and of the World to Come." In *Southern Baptists Observed*, ed. Nancy Ammerman. Knoxville: University of Tennessee Press, 1993.
Walzer, Michael. *Spheres of Justice: A Defense of Pluralism and Equality*. New York: Basic Books, 1983.
Weber, Max. *From Max Weber: Essays in Sociology*. Edited by H. H. Geerth and C. Wright Mills. New York: Oxford University Press, 1946.
———. *The Protestant Ethic and the Spirit of Capitalism*. 1904. Reprint. Translated by Talcott Parsons. New York: Charles Scribner's Sons, 1958.
———. *The Sociology of Religion*. 1922. Reprint. Translated by Ephraim Fischoff. Boston: Beacon Press, 1956.
Wiebe, Robert. *The Search for Order, 1877–1920*. New York: Hill & Wang, 1967.
Wilson, Bryan. "An Analysis of Sect Development." *American Sociological Review* 24 (February 1959), 3–15.
Wuthnow, Robert. *The Restructuring of American Religion*. Princeton: Princeton University Press, 1988.

Index